DOUBLE YOUR INCOME IN 1 YEAR OR LESS
(USING REAL ESTATE INVESTMENT STRATEGIES)

TABLE OF CONTENTS

INTRODUCTION

You've heard the stories! People on late-night infomercials telling you about fixing up properties and selling them for profit. Well, the truth is that you can make money using those very strategies (and it's hard work). But, there is a better way to do it. It's lower risk and with a smaller amount of effort from the Buy, Fix and Sell Method.

Of course, anything you do will take time, effort and energy. What you want to do is work smart and reduce the potential risks while increasing your upside potential.

You see, the problem with these infomercial programs is that they require a lot of time and money. How are you going to find the contacts or people with money while keeping your nose to the grindstone for the employer that allows you to put food on the table (you want excitement? – tell your employer that you need a paid leave of absence so you can go out and get started in real estate investment which will allow you to quit your employment). Obviously, quitting your full-time job is not the answer.

And this doesn't even address that matter of time. Do you dare neglect you current money-making activities to learn the complex methods and strategies that these programs require?

What do you need? What you need is a means of breaking into real estate investment that needs a **small amount of capital** from you!

Is that really possible, or is it just more hype?

Keep reading and see. This doesn't mean you can just do it any old way. There are certain fundamental principles involved. But if you do things the correct way, it can work. It involves working smarter and putting in the proper effort and motivation as well.

So, what's the trick?

We mentioned certain fundamental principles that lead to success. Here is one that applies here and helps you make money without spending money and without putting yourself at a lot of risk:

Strategy: You don't need to own a property to make money on it, you just need to have control over it.

What are your goals in real estate (both short term and long term):

_____

_____

_____

_____

_____

_____

_____

_____

Chapter 1 – Wholesaling: Make $500-$5,000 in 30 days or less!

Real-Life Example #1:

We'll look at an example first, then the explanation afterwards. J.K. of Hartford, CT. caught the real estate investor bug while in college. He bought a beat-up old mobile home to live in, and over time painted, re-carpeted and generally made it pretty. When he graduated, he sold it for $5,000 more than he paid for it. He liked that so much that he decided to make investing his central occupation. The first deal he went after was a 6-unit apartment building in downtown Hartford. The price was great – unbelievably low. It turns out the reason for the low price was that the building had been involved in a fire. Evidently the owners at the time had failed to insure the structure and were forced into a fire-sale price.

It's always good to get a low price on a deal, but, the cost might be more that the sales price. In this case, our friend brought in a contractor to make an estimate on the needed repairs. Cost of repairs came out to $75,000. That was much more than this recent graduate of U-Conn had available to him. He was clearly in over his head.

But J.K. was smart enough to know that he didn't have to walk away from the deal. He knew that the purchase contract that he had with the owners of the apartment building gave him control over the property. How?

- A **real estate purchase contract** provides the "Buyer" under the contract with the legal right to buy the property for the price stipulated within the time-frame given in the contract.
- Nobody else may legally purchase that property for the life of the contract without getting say-so from the buyer under the contract.
- The buyer under the contract will gladly give say-so formally and in writing for a fee.

In this case, J.K. advertised the apartment building for sale in the two major Hartford daily newspapers for the price contracted for. As we mentioned before, this was an excellent price. This generated a good volume of callers. One of the callers was a general building contractor with both the capital and the crew to rehabilitate the building. J.K. assigned his interest in the purchase contract to the builder for $4,000.

This is a true Win/Win situation. J.K. got $4,000 for his ability to find a deal and negotiate a contract. The builder got a great project without having to hit the bricks to find it: now his employees have work and he will make a lot of money off the building, either by selling it after the work is done or holding it for the on-going cash flow from rentals. The sellers got rid of the building that they couldn't afford to repair.

Bottom line: J.K. did not spend a penny to make $4,000. He didn't lift a single paintbrush. He incurred no risk. In fact, in the unlikely event he was unable to find anyone to take the purchase contract off his hands, he would have evoked one of the contingency clauses in the contract that would have cancelled the deal with no further recourse to him.

No Money, Working Smart, Proper Motivation and Limited Risk!

Notes:

_____

_____

_____

_____

_____

Real-Life Example #2:

A.D. lives and works in a mid-western city. He decided he didn't like his job that much and wanted to expand out. It wasn't an awful job, but, he wanted more. If you don't like what you do, any activity can be a job.

So, he decided to try real estate investing. Problem was he didn't have much money. So he decided to apply the principle we are talking about here. He set out to gain control of properties without owning them in order to make money. We'll look at the details of what he did later on, but, first let's look at the results.

Simply put, A.D. put the word out that he was looking for rental houses owned by out-of-state owners. An out-of-state owner called him. This man owned a house in a fairly desirable area that he was renting to the tenants from hell. They hadn't paid rent in two months. The property was trashy and beat up. The carpets were filthy, the yard was neglected. The owner's sense of distress came over the phone loud and clear.

It appeared that with some cosmetic work the house would be worth about $75,000. It needed paint, carpeting and wallpaper about $5,000 worth. The owner was renting the house out for $600 a month. In that neighborhood that kind of house should have rented for $750 so the actual rent seemed low. The mortgage balance was $55,000. Payments of $550 a month included taxes and insurance. By the time the owner spoke with A.D., he had already made two mortgage payments without getting any rent from his tenants.

One man's problem, A.D.'s opportunity –

What A.D. proposed not only solved the out-of-state landlord's problem, but, created a very nice payday for A.D., as well. Their agreement had A.D. rent the house for $550 a month for a two-year term. This amount covered the out-of-state owner's mortgage payments. He further agreed to get rid of the current tenant, sparing the owner one more hassle and expense. Together with a lease, A.D. received an option from the owner to purchase the house within the two-year term. The amount of the purchase happened to be the balance of the mortgage at the time. In other words, the out-of-state relieved him of a money-losing situation with no further financial loss.

Anita John

Let's recap what the two agreed to……

Lease term: 2 years
Monthly rent: $550
Purchase Option: $55,000

On the surface, this is a decent enough deal. A.D. had the property tied up for two years and was paying a rent amount lower than the going rate. Even better, he had the right to buy the house well below the market price.

There were a few challenges A.D. needed to take care of:

➢ He had inherited un-cooperative tenants;
➢ The property needed repairs, and;
➢ It would still require cash to buy this place in two years, which he didn't have.

Most people think that getting bad tenants out is very difficult, but, in this case it was easier than you might think. Everything anybody does is based either on anticipation of pleasure or avoidance of pain. The easiest way to evict a tenant is to make leaving very attractive. Problem tenants can suddenly become quite cooperative when it's to their benefit. Often that means cash. In this case, A.D. simply knocked on the door and asked them to leave. They did without fuss! (Had they not, there were other options, such as offering to let the two months un-paid rent slide if they are gone tomorrow).

Now was the issue of the repairs. To complicate things, A.D. had spent his last $100 as consideration for the agreement with the out-of-state owner.

His solution? He simply sub-leased the property to a handyman. In exchange for the work performed on the property, he would give the tenant an option to buy the property from him. This action concept led, of course, to the third problem to be solved. He couldn't sell the property to the new tenant until it was his to sell. He only had control, remember, not ownership.

Sometimes you just have to make a leap of faith. We will see later on how this worked to make A.D. a lot of money. But first of all, he took action. He ran an ad in the paper:

RENT-TO-OWN
Low down. U-fix
Large House
Call 555-9876

The simple ad generated a large volume of calls! A.D. considered the candidates and picked one particularly nice couple that was willing to fix the house up. A.D. proposed $1,500 option (earnest) money and $750 a month rent. Of the $750 a month, $200 would serve as a rent credit towards their down payment, combined with the $1,500 earnest money. With the agreement, the couple now had option to purchase the property for $75,000. They countered with the proposal to pay $3,500 now and $575 a month rent. The larger sum up front was very attractive and that became their agreement.

The couple was in the house before A.D. even owed a first rent payment to the owner. They cleaned up the property and steam-cleaned the carpets. Here A.D. was expecting to have to replace the carpets, but, this couple decided that they were fine with them as long as they were clean. Think about it! Who's going to live there? If the buyer is happy, why do any more? They actually like the ugly wall paper and the re-pained a few rooms, at their own expense.

Things were moving along well for A.D. $100 paid to the owner of the house and $30 for a newspaper ad were his total expenses. He had $3,500 cash in hand. He was making an extra $25 a month on the difference between the rent he paid the owner and what his tenants paid him.

Notes:

_____

_____

_____

_____

_____

_____

_____

_____

_____

_____

_____

But what about problem number three?

Problem number 3 actually had two parts:

a. How can he pay the owner for the house in order to give the tenants clear title when they buy?
b. How are the tenants going to buy? They have a poor credit history, including a bankruptcy and some collections.

A soon as he could, A.D. contacted a local mortgage broker and asked about the tenants' chances of getting of loan. He wasn't really worried, since their $3,500 was ***non-refundable.*** He couldn't lose, really. If they buy, he gets the rest of the money. If they don't buy, he still collected the $3,500.

The mortgage broker reviewed the tenants' financial situation and reported back to A.D. that he could get them financing.

Indeed, even a person with a bankruptcy on their record can get a mortgage loan knowing that the interest rate would be elevated to secure the lenders' risk! We will come back to this point later on, because knowing how credit works can help you get a lot of eager buyers into homes that you have control over. Who is going to be easier to please, after all, the couple with perfect credit who know they can get any kind of loan, or the people who think lenders will throw them out the door and call out the dogs on them? You help them finance the house you make available to them on terms they can qualify for, and you become a hero. Heroes get paid well in our society. But we'll cover the workings of credit later.

Let's go back to our example for now. A.D. worked closely with the lender and the tenants for the next 6 months. It took dozens of phone calls, but, finally an approval came. The tenants had financing!

A.D. immediately called the out-of-state owner and let him know about the upcoming closing. The owner was thrilled, because he had rid himself of a huge financial drain and a worry. He signed over the deed and received a check from the title company for $55,000.

Then A.D. sat down with the tenants. He could now give them a deed. He had just received it from the owner, who was already on his way home, a very happy man. The mortgage lender provided the $75,000 purchase price (minus the $3,500 the tenants had already paid). The title company handed A.D. a check for $16,500 (the amount left over after the title company paid $55,000 to the former owner of the property). A.D. walked away from the deal with $20,000 net cash profit, which included the $100 he paid to get the option from the out-of-state owner.

Three FLIP Strategies

Let's look at three lessons to learn from the two examples we have seen so far:

You Don't Own Investment Property, Just Control It

Owning property is great if you don't have to pay for it. Years ago there were lots of "non-qualifying" FHA and VA loans and assumptions. It was easy to buy, fix and sell. Things are different now. Banks don't want to lend money so easily and certainly not for extended terms. Even if you have lots of cash, you'll eventually run out.

You Don't Need To Borrow Money From Banks to Buy Houses

Banks prefer short-term business loans to long-term financing. They also have many regulations imposed on them that restrict their flexibility. Even if you qualify for a mortgage on the basis of credit history and personal income, they may not offer terms that meet your needs. Besides, why take out a mortgage if you don't intend to hold onto the property for more than a couple of months? **If you do borrow money make sure they don't charge pre-payment penalties.**

You Don't Need To Fix Up Houses, Focus on the Financing

In both these stories, the investors never performed any physical work on the house. They solved somebody else's problem and created desirable terms that allowed a third party to take over ownership of the property. The third party was happy to fix up the property.

J.K. bailed out a building owner who had foolishly neglected to provide insurance and was facing financial disaster while delivering a highly desirable product for the building contractor to buy and profitably use.

A.D. solved a money-drain problem for a man a thousand miles away while helping a young couple finally realize the American dream and own their own home.

Both J.K. and A.D. got paid for the services they rendered and the solutions to problems they provided, not for the sweat of their brows. The opportunity to render service and solve problems came because they were alert enough to see them and because they took action. The opportunity was not for sale, so they did not have to buy anything.

Here is an important principle of really building wealth:

You can have anything you desire, if you help enough other people get what they need.

What does This All Mean For You?

As a beginning entrepreneur and/or real estate investor, capital represents one of the largest barriers you will face. It's easy to buy properties if you have cash and excellent credit and connections. Even then, leveraging your excellent credit many not be the smartest use of your money and credit.

You can see that it is possible to make up to $3,000 - $10,000 per month investing in real estate. In fact, you don't even have to know how to replace a roof or fix bad plumbing. None of that should concern you at this point. Those who get the opportunity to own a home from you can take care of the repairs for you.

**FLIPS are a creative method to make money in real estate
Without having to buy the property.**

So how do you get started?

The two examples we read utilize two different techniques. To start, then, let's look into how the two techniques work. The fundamental concept is the same; the execution is slightly different in each case.

But before we outline the differences, let's look at some common points – some fundamental principles that apply to real estate investing across the board, whether you buy or not.

1- As a real estate entrepreneur, you don't always look for particular properties; you look for highly motivated sellers.

Other than the obvious fact that this works best with single family homes, the most important qualification of the seller is that the seller be very eager to take care of things. If the seller has a problem, you can provide a solution. Your solution ensures your payday. It's that simple. On the other hand, if the seller were not highly motivated, it would be easier for you (and probably less painful, in the long run) to just find a brick wall to beat your head against. It's so simple: motivated seller + motivated entrepreneur (you) = a good deal.

How do you suppose A.D. was able to gain control of a $75,000 house with only $100? The guy in out of state was at his wits end; he was hemorrhaging cash each month and would continue to do so until someone bailed him out. The apartment building owner in Connecticut had hundreds of thousand of dollars on the line; you can bet the mortgage was still due while the apartment was barely habitable.

Point #1 – Look for a highly motivated seller.

2- As an investor, whom you know is almost as important as what you know.

There are several people and types of people who you should have in your contact database:

a. ***Other Investors***

Never think of other investors as competition. Rarely will you run head-to-head with another investor on a deal. More than likely, other investors will work with you in a variety of roles:

> Mentors
> Joint venture partners
> Money partners
> People to sell from
> People to obtain deals from

b. ***People looking for a place to buy***

If you know that Jim and Suzy would like to find a little 3 bedroom, 1 bath house to buy and start their family in, wouldn't it make be a lot easier for you to make, offer and negotiate a purchase contract on a 3 bedroom, 1 bath house in the neighborhood they like, knowing that they will take it off your hands? Not only will they take it off your hands, they will pay for having found it and negotiating a good price for them. The key here is knowing to whom you can show the deal to once you find it.

c. *Your personal support team*

Do you really want to do everything yourself? Learn to delegate. Some things aren't worth you doing (you can make more money doing other things), other things you don't have the expertise to do, and other things you simply don't have time to do. Check out a description of the people that make up your team later in this manual.

Point #2 – Noone is an island!

Let's examine the key fundamentals.

We will look at two activities designed to allow you to make money in real estate without the need of ever purchasing property yourself. As we showed above, because you provide a valuable service to others, you get paid. These two activities are:

> **Contract flips**
> **Sandwich lease options**

Different people might use different names, but, the activities are broadly seen as some of the least risky and easiest ways to make money. If you hear the term "wholesaling," this is what they're talking about. Sometimes, however, people might talk about flipping, but, they mean purchasing the house, then selling it again quick after fix-up. This obviously entails certain elements that we wish to avoid here: financing, purchase, fix-up, risk, worry and hassle...... You get the picture?

Mind you, there is nothing wrong with purchasing a property, fixing it up pretty and selling quickly. There's a lot of money there. However, we suggest you wait until your flips and lease options accumulate enough capital for you to do it without worry.

So here's what to do:

Simply put, a contract can be assigned. That means that if you are the buyer under a contract to purchase and sell real property, you can assign your rights under the contract to a third party. Assuming that the contract represents a good deal for the buyer, giving up your buyer rights means you are giving up something of value. For that you deserve to be compensated. Conversely, the assignee – the person to whom you assign these rights, gains some of value, which must be paid for.

There is no set amount for the assignment fee. It can be considered as more than a finder's fee, since you not only find the property but also negotiate a contract. It has a lot to do with the value of the property involved and can range on a small scale from $1,000 to $5,000 to $45,000 in higher market areas such as California and New York. This might become clearer as we look at what you actually do with a contract flip (see chapter 9 for more information on how this works).

Notes:

_____

_____

_____

_____

_____

_____

_____

_____

_____

_____

_____

_____

Chapter 2: Real Estate Contract and Assignment

What is a Contract?

A contract is an agreement between two or more persons (individuals, businesses, organizations, or government agencies) to do, or to refrain from doing, a particular thing in exchange for something of value.

What are the Key Elements to a Binding Real Estate Contract?

1. **Offer and Acceptance:** Original signatures with no alterations to the contract. If the original offer is marked up and initialed by the party receiving it, then signed, this is not an offer and acceptance but a counter-offer.

2. **Consideration:** A bargained for exchange of something of value. Money is the most common form of consideration, but, a promise to perform (i.e. a promise to pay) is also satisfactory.

3. **In Writing:** A real estate contract must be in writing and it must:
   - Identify the Parties: The full name of the parties must be on the contract.
   - Identify the Property: At least the address, but, preferably the legal description must be on the contract, (i.e. Block #, Lot #)
   - Purchase Price: The amount of the sales price or a reasonably ascertainable figure (an appraisal to be completed at a future date) must be on the contract.
   - Signatures: A real estate contract must be signed to be enforceable.
   - Legal Purpose: The contract is void if it calls for illegal action.
   - Competent Parties: Minor, mentally impaired, drugged persons, etc. cannot enter into a contract.
   - Meeting of the Minds: Each side must be clear as to the essential details, rights and obligations of the contract.

What is a Lease Purchase Contract?

A lease purchase contract combines a basic lease contract with an option-to-purchase contract. The tenant/buyer pays to the landlord/seller a non-refundable option deposit that is applied to the purchase price of the home. The tenant/buyer then pays to the landlord/seller a sum that is typical to the renter amount usually on a monthly basis. A portion of that monthly payment is then applied to the purchase price of the home. During, or at the end of the lease period, the tenant/buyer has exclusive right to buy the home under the terms to which both parities have previously agreed.

In other words, Lease + Option to Purchase = Lease Option.

Show that house off!

Do you want to have tenants fighting to lease purchase your home? Sure you do! What landlord doesn't? Listen up and let me show you how to accomplish this magical feat.

Here is a list of critical things that you must do at every open house if you want to have people literally begging to lease purchase your home:

➢ A fresh baked apple pie or some chocolate chip cookies smell delicious, are nice touch and make your home smell wonderful.

➢ Brew a pot of fresh coffee so you can offer it to your guests. Cut and trim the grass, edge the sidewalks and trim the bushes. This will help to give your home curb appeal, which is absolutely essential to attracting tenant/buyers.

➢ Clean clutter from your yard, deck, driveway, garden, garage and even the street. Also clean your gutters and roof. This will also help to give your home curb appeal.

➢ Make the front entryway sparkle. Since this is where people will enter your home, the first impression they get from the front door and entry way are very important to lease purchasing your home. You may even want to put a fresh coat of paint on your front door or buy some nice plants to display.

➢ Clean the kitchen; take out the garbage, clear the countertops of clutter. Clean all dirty dishes and put them away, wipe down the appliances and sweep and mop the floors.

➢ Clean the bathrooms; empty the wastebaskets, clean and organize the countertops, put personal items away, scrub the toilet and tub/shower, sweep and mop the floors and clean the mirrors.

➢ Clean the bedrooms; clear all the clutter from the floors and vacuum/sweep them, make the beds, organize the dresser drawer tops, dust the furniture, lamps and blinds and organize the closets.

➢ Make the family and dining rooms sparkle; pick up clutter from the floors and vacuum/sweep them, dust the furniture, electronics, blinds and lamps, clear or organize all tables and arrange blankets and throw pillow neatly.

➢ Wash windows and any other glass around the house and straighten any pictures or wall ornaments.

➢ Light some scented candles to create that intimate atmosphere.

➢ Tie balloons to a yard sign or mailbox to more easily identify your home to passers by.

➢ Buy some fresh flowers and display them throughout your house, but, definitely put them on your dining room or kitchen table.

➢ Turn the television off and play some classical music at a low volume.

What we are trying to create is a welcome, comfortable, hospitable feeling that will cause any person to immediately fall in love with your home. If you follow the advice given above, you should have your home lease purchased in lightning speed.

Notes:

_____

_____

_____

_____

_____

_____

_____

_____

_____

_____

_____

Chapter 3: Lease Options – How Do They Work?

Investing in real estate can be immensely rewarding, but, it can also be scary. Given the large sums of money involved, it is easy for the investor to worry about what will happen if nobody wants the property that has cost so much – or what if the costs amount to more than the profit?

Conventional wisdom looks at two general types of real estate investments: those that an investor buys to flips, or to sell again for a quick cash return and those that one acquires to rent out for long-term cash flow. Both are good; having both kinds creates diversity in the investment portfolio. Immediate income capitalizes the business.

Both have potential problems, too. If an investor has acquired a home at 90% of its market value with the intent of fixing it up for resale that means carrying costs: mortgage payments to the funding source, property taxes, insurance, selling expenses. On a $100,000 home, this could easily amount to a monthly outflow in excess of $800 while waiting for the house to sell and then close. Not only is the $800 a month likely to be a burden, but the $2,400+ paid in three months represents nearly a fourth of the projected profit on the deal and the rest will be eaten up in 6% agent commissions and the closing costs. Why go through the bother only to break even?

Renting has its own hazards. Let's say that by paying $800 a month on this house, one can't rent it for $900. Cash flow is $100 a month and the property will appreciate over the years. What happens, however, if the tenant moves out and it takes a month to get a new one in? What happens if the first renter was the tenant from hell, who punched holes in the walls, let five dogs relieve themselves regularly on the living room carpet and takes the refrigerator with him? Once again, the investor pays $2,000 for the privilege of clearing $100 a month.

What we need is an alternative that doesn't cost as much as flipping a property but generates more income than renting. The alternative: lease-option.

What is least-option? It starts with a normal lease agreement, signed for a home for a set period of time. The tenant makes monthly rent payments and the landlord supplies the tenant a place to live.

With a lease option, we add an additional step, an option agreement, which gives the tenant the privilege of purchasing the house within a given time period for a price agreed upon in advance.
It is easy to see that a lease option is a hybrid of the two ways of dealing with a property that we described above – renting and flipping. As you will see, however, it mitigates most of the risks involved with these two methods while retaining many of the advantages.

Let's look at some advantages of ***lease-option*** over renting:

> ➢ Instead of collecting a refundable deposit and the first month rent up front, you collect the rent plus a non-refundable option consideration of anywhere from $1,000 to $10,000, depending on your market.

> ➢ Instead of collecting the normal market monthly rent payments, you get rent plus an additional amount. You credit the additional amount toward the option as further non-refundable consideration *(since this is non-refundable, it is yours to keep as profit, even if the deal is never completed and the tenant never exercises the option).*

➢ At the time the option is exercised, you receive the remainder of the profit you have coming to you, based on your earlier estimate of what the market value of the house would be at the end of the option term.

➢ Your tenant is planning on buying the house; whom do you suppose will take better care of it, the renter who plans on moving on eventually, or the tenant who wants to own it? In other words, your investment property is well taken care of.

➢ The option agreement stipulates that the tenant becomes responsible for maintenance. Instead of calling you in the middle of the night when the sewer backs up, the tenant calls Roto Rooter and pays for the service without deducting it from the rent.

In short, you get more money up front more money during the course of the lease, a profit on the back end, the tenant takes better care of the property and assumes responsibility for maintenance. On top of that, as you will see in our next installment, the investor can turn this property around in just a couple of weeks instead of in several months.

What is the best way to market a house for a lease option? First, let's look at the target market. Who might be interested in a minimal down payment to buy a house? Think of a *young married couple, newlyweds.* Between the two of them, they make enough to handle the payments, but, they haven't had time to save up for a down payment for a conventional loan. This is all the more the case if they *just got out of college*. Between the two of them, they may be earning $4,000 a month, but, have *no savings*. However, they feel the need to invest in a place to live and know that if they had to, they could scrape up $3,000 from various relatives. There are other people who have been married for a number of years, but have been living paycheck to paycheck and have never saved anything, or they have a credit history that makes conventional financing too expensive.

What will catch their attention? First of all, an announcement – *RENT TO OWN!* –Will make a strong impression. The term, "lease option," may be incomprehensible jargon to them, but, "rent to own" they are familiar with. Who knows, maybe that's how they furnished their apartment. This is then the foundation of our advertising.

The ads we place might be newspaper classified (or classifieds in the Penny Savers from the convenience store), or they might be fliers posted in public places. Both will work. For double coverage, you could place classifieds both in the *Homes for Sale* and *Homes for Rent* section of the paper. Here are possible ads you can run:

RENT TO OWN
Nice 3-bedroom home,
Owner desperate, must sell, $3,000 gets
You in.
555-1234.

When people call, *don't make the mistake of seeing people separately*. Half of them won't show up, and you will experience the frustration of driving over to this house and waiting for 45 minutes for nothing. Instead, *try this 5-minute dialogue when they call you*:

"Hi, I'm calling about this house in the paper, rent to own."
"Oh yes, thanks for calling. Which ad was that?"

"It says, '$3,000 gets you in'."

"Great! I'd like to show it to you. Do you have the $3,000?" (Or: "Can you handle the $900 a month?")

"Yes."

"How's your credit?"

"It's o.k."

"Good. I'll tell you what. I'm going to be over at the house this Saturday to clean things up. Meet me at 4:00, I'll show you through and let you fill out a credit application. Bring your checkbook for the deposit, and I'll see you there."

Saturday at 4:00 there should be a pretty good crowd at the house, wandering around the yard, peering in the windows, wondering where you are. About 10 after the hour you show up and apologize for being late. Then look at your clip board (where you have a list of the people you talked to on the phone, having marked the ones that sounded certain to be there) and ask, OK, now who's Ed and Lucille?" Ed and Lucille steps forward, you say, "come on, I'll show you through." Then say to the rest, "this will just take a minute and I'll be right back to take care of the rest of you. Just hold on a minute, OK?"

You let the first couple look at your house and then have them fill out a credit application in the kitchen. (The kitchen is generally the room that makes or breaks the deal). Take the application and their check for $3,000 and say, "It'll take me 10 to 15 days to check this out, but, then I'll get back to you." They leave, you get the next couple.

Note: you may be concerned about asking for $3,000 from strangers – why would they be willing to give that much to someone they don't know? Here's why? There are 10 other couples standing out on your front lawn willing to pay $3,000, and they know it. They recognized an opportunity to get a place of their own in a way they can afford to. For that matter, if they don't want to pay $3,000, go ahead and say: "you know, I can understand that and I respect that. Here, we'll put the credit app in the trash. Don't worry about it." Many will give in at that moment; others will suddenly change their minds out on the driveway after they leave the house. If they don't, so what. You have 10 other couples eager to buy your house.

We recommend taking the deposit up front from 2-3 only:

➤ You know a person who gives you a check is committed and you don't have to worry about doing all that due diligence on all those credit applications for nothing.

➤ Then you deposit the 1st check in the order received and refund those who did not get the house.

➤ Hopefully, you'll have more than one house so repeat the above referenced cycle with possibly no additional costs for classified advertising -- especially in light of social networking such as Craigslist, Twitter, Facebook, etc...

Regarding payments, the investor has a strong device for ensuring prompt lease payments. Remember, the lease payment is made up of a base rent amount (normal for the local market) and an extra sum for option consideration. If they pay on time (let's say, before the 3rd of the month), the extra amount counts. After the 3rd, the extra amount is just part of the rent. You get the same amount regardless, but, if they pay late, then end up owing more down payments at the end.

How To Protect a Lease Option

There are some things you should take care of to protect a lease option. One thing you want to avoid is a situation known as an ***equitable mortgage.*** In brief, that means that a judge decides that your arrangement is not a lease but a mortgage. This might come about if you have a bad tenant, whom you wish to evict, but, who protests in court this is really a purchase, therefore you must foreclose. With an eviction, you can get the person out often times within a month; a foreclosure means nine months with no lease income. Here are things you can do to ensure this is not a problem. **Always consult a real estate lawyer before signing any legal documents**:

> ➤ Know the landlord-tenant law for your state.
> ➤ Record the option agreement for public record.
> ➤ Escrow the deed with an escrow or title company.
> ➤ Keep the lease agreement and the option agreement as ***two separate documents.***
> ➤ Keep the terms relatively short – two years (or less) is good.
> ➤ Take a refundable security deposit (a small amount so that the tenant can still afford the non-refundable option consideration).
> ➤ Seller pays all property taxes and insurance (structure only) on the property.
> ➤ Don't give unusually large option credits as part of the monthly payment.
> ➤ **Watch contract language:**
>   **Good: landlord/tenant, non-refundable option consideration.**
>   **Avoid: buyer/seller, credit towards down payment.**

In summary, a lease-option is a possibility for dealing with a property that doesn't leave you enough equity that you want to risk flipping it or just renting.

Options as a way to gain control over a property

Tips for Starters to Truly Use the Lease Purchase Contract

Lease options as a means of gaining control over a property is a relatively non-risky way of making money in real estate, as long as you do it correctly. We have compiled a few points here to help you structure your agreements right for less hassle and fewer problems.

Tip #1 – Be a smart and a good landlord

Landlords are creditors. Think of that. They let people live in their property in trust that they will get paid. As a creditor, you should make good use of the credit tools available to you. Make sure you screen your tenant/buyers properly to avoid problems with them in the future. As the landlord/ seller, the two major concerns that you will face are collecting rent on time and the destruction of your property. These risks can be greatly reduced, if not eliminated, with a little research.

Minimize Your Risk
> ➤ Have the tenant/buyer fill out a **detailed rental application**.
> ➤ Check the tenant/buyer's **credit history**.
> ➤ Make an un-announced visit to the tenant/buyer at their current residence to see how well they maintain it. What you see there is what you will see at your home.

> ➤ Call previous landlords to verify payment history, quality of tenants, etc. If a previous landlord is reluctant to reveal any information for fear of liability, simply ask, "Would you rent to this tenant again?" Now they can be honest without fear. Incidentally, the current landlord may not be a good source; if this is the tenant from hell, he or she might tell you anything you want to hear to get relief.
> ➤ Verify the tenant/buyer's employment.
> ➤ Ask for many references and check them.
> ➤ Get a large option deposit to create value in the tenant/buyer's mind.
> ➤ Make the tenant/buyer responsible for the maintenance.
> ➤ Use your instincts.

Why is this so important? Because you want to focus all of your time creating new opportunities and enjoying life to it's fullest – not worrying about tenants.

Tricks of the Trade

Here are a few ideas to create a good rapport with tenants who hold an option to buy. It's not necessary to become their drinking buddies, but, people generally destroy rental property out of hostility toward the landlord who owns it. If the tenants have good feelings toward the landlord, they generally pay promptly, behave better and keep things cleaner and in better repair:

> ➤ Encourage tenant/buyers to allow automatic transfer from their account to yours.
> ➤ Coincide rent due dates with tenant/buyer's paydays.
> ➤ Send your tenant/buyer a holiday, birthday or better yet, a Thanksgiving card. How often do you receive Thanksgiving cards? They will definitely remember it.
> ➤ Tenant/buyer's who think like home buyers act in the following manner:
>   a. They take better care of your home
>   b. They pay rent on time and fulfill other obligations
>   c. They handle repairs and other maintenance improvements and upgrades on your home.
>   d. To create the appearance that they're actually homeowners, you should send them a monthly statement that shows their current amount due, due date, late payment fees and any notes you want to include.
> ➤ When signing a lease, give the tenant/buyer twelve-stick'em labels with your address printed on them. All they need to do is peel off one each month, place it on the envelope with a stamp and mail it.
> ➤ To encourage timely rental payments, on an addendum to the option to buy, state that the tenant/buyer will receive an option consideration bonus (maybe $1,500) if they make all of their monthly rental payments in a timely fashion. If they don't make their payments on time, declare the option consideration bonus void by sending written confirmation to that effect.
> ➤ In the first month, welcome the tenant/buyer as a "future home buyer" and use that term in both oral and written contact.
> ➤ Send an "on-time thank you voucher," valued at either $25 or $50 good towards the purchase of the home. If they are ever late, any vouchers received up to that point are considered null and void.
> ➤ While lease purchasing a home to a tenant/buyer, it would be to your benefit to give them a periodical checkup to see what progress they are making towards purchasing your home. You want them to be ready when the time comes.

An ounce of prevention really pays off and your home should be on automatic pilot.

Tip #2 – The Marketplace

Rent to own is not a fad. It is the the next creative real estate revolution that will affect the way you and your family work, live and play for the rest of your lives. According to the Association of Progressive Rental Organizations, the rental industry's trade association, the rent-to-own business is more than forty years old, generates about $4.4 billion in revenues for the industry and serves nearly three million customers. It shows no signs of slowing down, in fact, all indications point to increased revenues for years to come – especially with the advent of the lease purchase contract in real estate.

Until now it has been difficult for anyone who wants to buy, sell or invest in real estate to really make it a big success. Here are ways to make sure you are successful – just look at the previous success stories.

The lease purchase is second to no other form of financing. Look at those people who sell their home with seller financing. First, they give up title to their home and transfer it to the buyer. Then they take back a second mortgage note, which is junior and subordinate to the first mortgage granted by a bank or mortgage company. If there are future problems with payments, they will have to go head-to-head with a well-funded financial institution and its army of attorneys to try and salvage any of their rights as creditors. They start the process at a huge disadvantage because the mortgage they hold is subordinate to the bank's paper. Besides, if they did have to foreclose to get their property back, it is a time-consuming process (a year or more) and requires an expensive attorney to do it.

Contrast this with a lease option sale. You do not give up ownership or control of the house until you get paid *in full*. Failure to pay means you evict, not foreclose. The option agreement is tied to the lease so that default of the lease means default of the option. Once you evict the previous tenants, you simply place new tenants in the house who pay you the normal option consideration up front. If rents have gone up in the neighborhood, the new tenants pay the new higher amount.

So not only are you offering something that will attract attention, especially among first-time home buyers who do not have a down payment saved up or who lack the excellent credit needed for the best financing packages, but you are making things easier on yourself, as well. This is a Win/Win situation for both you and your broker/tenants.

Tip #3 – Offering Value and Asking for the Sale

When you place a tenant/buyer in a house, you complete a sales transaction. You have sold them on the concept of obtaining this house on your terms. That makes it very important to remember why people buy anything. Why do people buy?

People buy because of a perception of need, based on their feelings of what the product or service will do for them.

Always remember that people never buy a product or service because of its features (the factual information). Rather, people will buy a product or service because of the **benefits** they get from its features. For example, you wouldn't buy a home because it has a large yard, a washer and dryer and a two-car garage. But you would buy a home if your children will be safe and have a great time playing in the large yard. Knowing that you will have more free time because you don't have to go to the Laundromat to do your laundry will generate action from you. Knowing that the garage protects your cars from vandals, damaging elements or save you from scraping ice of the windshield will get you excited. People care about what the product or service will do for them – the benefits.

Be sure to offer value in the form of benefits to your tenant/buyers or, if you are the tenant/buyer, be able to create the lease purchase deal and offer value to your landlord/seller. Understand your clients' needs and you can address them with benefits.

What do tenant/buyers need? For starters, the most common reason for buying with a lease option is because credit problems make it difficult to get the kind of financing that make immediate purchase possible. An option gives the tenant/buyer time to repair credit while actually accumulating a down payment.

The same type of mentality that makes people buy furniture rent-to-own makes them flock to lease options. That mentality is simply the "I want it *now*!" philosophy. People simply don't want to wait until the kids are nearly grown to buy a house, but, it's difficult to afford it when the kids are young.

How about getting the deal to offer?

The other side of the coin is getting a current owner to let you gain control over the property with an option of your own. Why would an owner/landlord want to do this?

Again, it's a matter of benefits and value. This value comes in many different forms: faster equity accumulation, top sales price – even if demand is low for the home, higher than usual rent, no realtor commissions, all with minimum cash out of pocket.

The owner/landlords you will be talking to are not offering a lease option when you come onto the scene. They are either trying to rent a house they own or they are living in the house now. If they are trying to rent it, it might be because they couldn't get it sold back when they bought their new house, or (even worse for them) got transferred to a different state, or else they inherited it, or at one time thought they wanted to be a landlord, but, don't how to do it right. The point is, now they are dissatisfied with the status quo.

Lease purchase deals are not found – they are created. Using negotiation as a tool for success, you can quickly and easily buy or sell any kind of real estate. We will explain some strategies for doing this below.

Ask for the sale. Let's say it again. **Ask for the sale.** You can increase your results by up to 50% or more by simply asking for the sale. Many top sales people understand and appreciate this simple method to increase their productivity. There is a fundamental rule to real estate success:

If you don't ask, you don't get.

If you really look at the profile of a homebuyer or seller, you'll find that these are people who are usually well educated, hard working and have some disposable income. Almost all of them have good jobs and pay their bills on time. Because they each have different needs and desires, it will be your job to determine exactly what problem they have and offer a solution to their problem – this is the power of the lease purchase contract. It is the most flexible creative finance technique available to any free market in the world today!

Tip #4 – Rewards, Value, Safety and Security

Creating a lease purchase deal can be very rewarding (both monetarily and mentally) if you do it right. Do you have any idea how quick and easy most lease purchase deals actually are? For example, you all have heard of rent-to-own furniture stores.

These companies serve over three million customers each year and generate over $4.4 billion in revenues.

These are some serious numbers.

You simply will not find a safer, more secured way to transfer ownership in real estate. We are reminded of a quote that attributed to The Great One, Wayne Gretzky, "You miss 100% of the shots you don't take." But you must have the proper knowledge in order to be successfully using the lease purchase contract.

Below are few examples of what you should know when it comes to buying, selling, renting, listing or investing in real estate. They are broken up into two categories; Features & Benefits and Marketing Tips.

Features & Benefits

The lease purchase contract is the quickest, easiest and least expensive way to buy, sell or invest in real estate. It replaces the typical adversarial relationship that usually exists between buyers and sellers with a win-win concept of transferring real estate ownership. As a result, it is highly sought after by those who are aware of its powerful features and benefits.

A Small Sample of <u>Landlord/Seller Benefits</u> (this is what it does for you):

- ➤ **<u>Top Sales Price</u>**, even if demand is low for the home: You attract to your home more tenant/ buyers who are willing to pay a premium because of the terms and value you are offering.
- ➤ **<u>Higher than Usual Rent</u>**: Since you are flexible on your terms and are offering value, you can demand a higher than usual rent.
- ➤ **<u>Positive Cash Flow</u>**: Since you can demand a higher than usual rent, this will increase your cash flow.
- ➤ **<u>Non-refundable Option Consideration Up Front = Minimum Risk</u>**: When a tenant/buyer executes (signs) a lease purchase contract, you receive and option deposit that is yours to keep if they default on the deal or decide not to buy.

- > **No Realtor Commissions**: Since your are selling your home yourself, you will avoid paying a 6%-10% Realtor commission. In the case of For-Sale-By-Owners, you save on advertising costs because you will have your home lease purchased more quickly.

- > **Attraction of the Highest Quality Tenants**: You are dealing with tenant/buyers who have a vested interest in the home, therefore, they think of themselves as homeowners and tend to take better care of it.

- > **Tax Shelter is maintained**. You remain on the deed until the option is exercised and consequently, you maintain all of the tax benefits of ownership.

- > **No Maintenance, No Land lording**: Tenants who have a vested interest and believe they are a homeowner may feel a "pride of ownership" that encourages them to pay on time, perform maintenance and make improvements to your home. Additionally, you can delegate maintenance to the tenant in your lease purchase agreement.

- > **Larger Market of Buyers**: You are marketing your home not only to buyers, but, also to renters and investors. These three groups make up 85% of those seeking to acquire real estate.

- > **No Long Vacancies**: Your phone will ring off the hook when you advertise your home is a lease/purchase deal. Typical turnover time is days or weeks, rather than months or years.

- > **Peace of Mind**: It is safer than conventional rentals because of the quality of the tenant/ buyers and their vested interest in your home. It also means that someone is living on-site who will watch and guard your home against vandalism, fire, etc.

A Small Sample of Tenant/Buyer Benefits:

- > **Faster Equity Growth**: Equity can accumulate exponentially faster than with conventional financing.

- > **Rent Money is Working Toward the Purchase of the Home:** Each month that you pay rent, a portion of that payment will be credited towards your down payment or off of the sales price.

- > **Option Consideration is Credited Towards the Purchase of the Home**: When you sign a lease purchase contract, you must pay the landlord/seller and option deposit. This money is your vested interest in the home and will be fully credited (100%) to either your down payment or off the sales price.

- > **Minimum Cash Out of Pocket**: When you purchase a home conventionally, you must pay closing costs, prepaid and a down payment. With a lease purchase, you pay only first month's rent and an option deposit. This will save you between 25% and 85%.

- > **Frequently No Down Payment at Closing**: Since you have given the landlord/seller an option deposit plus you have been receiving large monthly rent credits, there will frequently be very little or nothing left to come up with for a down payment at closing.

- > **Possible Assignment (Sale) of Contract for a Profit**: If you are allowed to assign your interest in the home, you may assign it to someone for a price.

➤ **Increased Buying Power**: Your buying power is dramatically increased. You can get into a lease purchase home for as little as first month's rent and a $1 option deposit.

➤ Compare that to a lender who requires 5-20% down plus closing costs and prepaid.

➤ **Credit problems are okay**: Qualification restrictions are not as strict as conventional financing. You will be approved at the sole discretion of the landlord/seller.

➤ **Control of the Home**: You will be put in full legal control of the home for a specified period of time without having to actually own it.

➤ **Maximum Leverage**: You are spending very little money to control a very expensive and potentially very profitable investment.

➤ **Time**: Before you actually buy the home, you will have time to repair your credit, find the best financing available, investigate the home and research the neighborhood.

➤ **Privacy**: Since you are leasing, there will be no public record of where you live (unless you record your option).

➤ **Peace of Mind**: You will have full control of the home and can maintain it or improve it however you wish.

Investor Benefits:

➤ As an investor, you're probably aware of the principles of leverage (the use of borrowed funds to improve one's capacity and to increase the rate of return on an investment). With the lease purchase contract, you can control properties that normally require 10-30% down for a nominal amount of money without using a lender or going through the loan application process.

➤ Additionally, the lease purchase contract is so quick and easy to use; you can dramatically increase your productivity and consequently, your cash flow. You will receive the same features and benefits as the landlord/seller or the tenant/buyer, depending on which role you take in your transactions.

There are literally dozens of different ways to use and market the lease purchase contract. You will learn which ones are the easiest, fastest and most effective; and which are a waste of your time. We will show you, step-by-step, how to make profits marketing your property with the lease purchase contract.

How Do You Find These Deals?

The signs are talking to you. Read Them!

When you see a "For Rent" sign on a single family home, you should just walk up to the home and knock on the door to see if anyone is home. If they aren't, that's okay. I just make note of the information on the sign with the landlord's phone number so I can make an appointment to visit the home or if this is an out of state owner, you can do everything online, visit www.fsbo.com . Pretend to be interested in renting the property so that you can get into it to do an A-Z inspection.

Before you go visit the property, however, **do your homework** go to www.zillow.com for comps/ estimated market value estimates. Find out how much similar properties in the neighborhood are selling for and then, after you have visited the property, ask the owner why he or she is renting instead of selling. You will discover that most of the time the owner is renting because he couldn't sell it and didn't know anything about lease purchasing!

Next ask the owner how much he or she wants for the property. If they give you a price below market value for the neighborhood, this is an excellent candidate because the owner is already willing to lease out the property. We simply can't think of a reason why the owner wouldn't want to do a lease option deal because they already told me they were interested in selling it.

Regarding properties that are being sold by Realtors, there is usually a sign in the yard. With these, simply get in touch with the owner of the property. **Inform them that when their contract with the Real Estate Company is terminated and if the property hasn't been sold, they should contact you immediately** also known as an expired listing. Explain that if they want to sell their property within 30 days, all they have to do is give you a call in order to make arrangements. **Give them your card with your name, telephone numbers, fax number and email address.**

These real estate signs really talk to you. Why? Because they inform you right away that the owner was willing to lose something like 7% on the selling price with the Real Estate Company that had the property listed. Can you imagine if the owner was also willing to lower the sales price?

Example: Asking price: $100,000 minus 7% for the RE commission = $93,000 let. Then let's say the owner lowers the price even more. WOW! The owner is losing a lot of money just because they don't know anything about lease option deals.

So for a deal like this, **simply make an offer around 5% less than the asking price and then listen to the owner for his or her answer**. What do you think?

Note that we suggest: "listen to the owner for his or her answer…" This is textbook sales technique. Since the success of your lease purchase business is somewhat dependent upon how good of a sales person you are, you will need to learn to **"BE QUIET", while you WFA (wait for an answer) after you've made your offer**. It sounds a little weird, but, by rambling on and on about how wonderful lease purchasing is, you talk them out of the deal. What comes out of their mouth next is very important. It will either be an objection (i.e. "sorry, I need all of my cash right now") or and acceptance of your offer. If it is an objection, you can overcome it.

Notes:

_____

_____

_____

_____

_____

_____

_____

_____

_____

_____

_____

Chapter 4: Sandwich Lease Options / No credit deals

How Can You Profit From A Sandwich?
A Property Investment and Low Capital Requirements

If a lease option is a good way for the investor to sell a house also a good way for the buyer who can't go through normal financing channels to buy a house, then doesn't it make sense that the investor could buy a house the same way? In fact, how about a way to gain control over a property without incurring the risks of actual ownership, while still making the same kind of profit?

The vehicle here is a sandwich lease option.

A sandwich lease option is simply two lease option arrangements sandwiched around a single investment transaction. You gain control over the property by signing an option agreement to buy it. You now control it because the owner cannot sell without first going to you. Your outlay on the deal might be as little as a security deposit and the first month's rent, possibly a little option consideration. Obviously, you will not volunteer to pay more consideration than the seller requires.

Meanwhile, you quickly place a tenant in the property using a separate lease option on the other side. Here you charge the normal option consideration, both up-front and monthly over the term of the agreed option, while requiring normal market rents.

What is your profit?

The full amount of the consideration (perhaps less your security deposit, unless you get a security deposit from your tenant to offset that – obviously your tenant at least offsets the rent you paid). Additionally, if your rent obligation is favorable enough, you can pick up a little on the margin between that and what your tenant pays you.

In short, this arrangement has its advantages:

> - The investor's capital costs can be minimized, since the property is not really purchased until the money comes in from the second half of the deal.
> - This can be done regardless of the investor's personal income or credit history.
> - Since the investor does not need financing, many of these deals can done simultaneously as the investor can find and negotiate.

Where do you find these deals?

To make it simple, don't bother with advertisements, classifieds or otherwise, for lease-options. The person who calls it that is savvy enough to pull all the potential profit out of the deal before you get to it. *Instead, approach landlords who advertise a house for rent, pure and simple, offline in the newspaper or online at www.fsbo.com.* All they want to do is get a tenant in before they stat losing money. However, many would welcome the chance to sell the house, too.

Why?

Why does a landlord rent out a single-family house? There are a few possible motives:

> ➤ The landlord is an investor who is holding onto it for cash flow.
> ➤ The landlord used to live in the house, then bought a new place and thought it would be cool to rent this one out; now it has become clear that that involves work and it's no longer fun.
> ➤ The landlord had to move because of a job transfer or just couldn't get the house sold when the new house was ready, so had to rent it out to offset the extra mortgage expense.

In any of these cases, the landlord might easily be persuaded that giving you an option would be smart business. In the last situation, persuasion probably won't be necessary; this is a highly motivated seller. At any rate, you can test it out with the following dialog:

FRBO: "Hi, I'm calling about the house you have for rent in Springfield. Can you tell me a little about it?"

After discussing it for a minute, continue:

YOU: "To tell you the truth, what I want to do is to buy a place, but, I can't afford to do so right now. But, I'd be very interested in renting this one from you with an option to buy it down the road a couple of years."

Now picture the reaction of the person who is tired of owning the house. You have just answered his or her prayers. Imagine if this person lives 1000 miles away now because of a job transfer. You are offering to relieve him or her of a major headache. Even better, what if the house has been vacant for two months when you call!

Note: Any time you spy a house for rent and see signs that nobody lives there nor has it been occupied for any length of time, stop the car, get out and talk to a neighbor. Find out the situation. Where is the owner? Why is it being rented? What happened to the last tenants? If the owner is out of state and had to rent it because it couldn't get sold in time, you have struck the mother lode. Call the owner and help him out of his/her misery. *Make sure you don't pay rent in a much higher amount than what is needed for the mortgage, taxes and insurance (yes, he/she still pays taxes and insurance, it's his/her house!).*

What if the owner is not interested?

If the landlord is interested in giving you an option, you can discuss the details at this time. If not, ask:

FRBO: "Oh, so are you an investor?"

Most likely this person is an investor wanting to hold onto the property. Use this opportunity to network with investors with whom you can do business with in the future. For example:

YOU: "That's great. I'm just learning right now and I've got ways to go, but, it's a lot of fun. Tell me, what kind of properties do you work with most? What works best for you?"

Give them an opportunity to play the expert, which they will most likely be happy to do. **Keep a database so that in the future**, if you come across a great 4-plex and you can buy it for time or money constraints, you could still get it under contract for a great price, then call those contacts like 4-plexes and explain:

YOU: "Hi, this is A. John. I talked to you a few weeks ago about your rental house over on Maple Avenue. You mentioned that you are looking for 4-plexes. Well, I've got a 4-plex under contract on South Jefferson with a pretty good price, but, some things have come up that will make it impossible for me to go through with the deal. Before I let it go, I wanted to see if you'd be interested in taking it off my hands."

The consideration on the assignment here could net you $3,000 - $5,000 for being able to negotiate a good purchase contract.

Here are some things to watch out for:

1. *Make sure that the lease agreement you sign as tenant doesn't prohibit you from sub-leasing.* Think about it for a moment and you will understand why. Remember this about sub-leasing. A primary reason for this prohibition is because the landlord is looking at this as a long-term investment and in the interest of preserving its value wishes to control who lives there, not cede that power to a third party. However, in this case, you have now taken over interest in the long-term investment and you desire this control for yourself.
   Besides, as you may have to explain, without striking that clause from the contract, you cannot do the deal. Highly motivated sellers will give in.
   Solution: **If you prepare the lease agreement, make sure it <u>makes no mention of sub-leasing.</u>**

2. Make sure you take in more money than you spend on the transaction. This may seem like a no-brainer, but, that is why you avoid the people advertising a lease option. Go to those who are only thinking of renting out the house. Ideally you want to pay a no option consideration. Maybe you end up paying $1,000 up front and nothing per month. Then you collect $2,000 from your tenant and $250 per month. Remember, the landlord was not thinking consideration when he placed the rental ad. Also, negotiate the lowest possible rent payments for yourself, so that you have a margin between what you pay and what you collect. It helps that you don't have to pay property taxes and insurance out of your rental revenues.

3. <u>**Set expiration for the option you give to be two month prior to the option you buy.**</u> If your tenant exercises the option, things will take care of themselves with a simultaneous or double closing. If the tenant doesn't exercise the option, you have three possibilities for your next move.
   - The tenant walks away from it, so do you. The option gives you the right to buy the house, not the obligation.
   - Tell the owner, "I thought I had things set up to buy this from you next month, but, that just fell through. I'd still like to do it though. Would you be interested in renewing the option for another two years?" For the past two years, you paid like clockwork and the house is in marvelous shape. Why wouldn't the owner want to continue?
   - You like the house; you have a two-month window, go out and get financing to buy the house under the original option terms.

Obviously this latter choice is the reason for the two-month difference.

A sandwich lease option is a good alternative to the normal buy-fix-sell type of lease option or flip. The advantage is that if you are currently cash-poor and over-extended, you're not out of business. Just rent a two-year investment, earn some of it now and make the rest later.

Find a tired landlord, find a good deal!

Here is a great technique that allows you to gain access to tired landlords and close more lease option deals.

Step 1: Run the following classified ad: "Problem Tenants? Call the Eviction Specialists. Simple. Easy. VERY effective. 555-4321.

Step 2: People will call asking about your services. Gain some rapport and then set up a time with them to meet and discuss exactly what their tenant problem is and how you can help them. The phone is NOT the time for details. (Remember, 80% + or our communication is non-verbal, meaning most of our communication comes from body language, facial expressions, gestures, even our aura: all you have on the phone is words and tone of voice).

Step 3: You meet with the landlord and you LISTEN to all of his or her problems: no rent in four months, the place is getting trashed; the tenants are dealing drugs, etc. Let them talk. You control the direction of the conversation by asking questions, so you should be the asker, not the teller at this point. After you have all of the details and the landlord has vested, you can explain how you can help:

You: "Mr. Jones, I am certain we can help you but I guess I have some other concerns here… and I know I may be overstepping my bounds so please don't be offended… but… What are you going to do the next time this happens? I mean this problem is bad enough but you know it often is part of the game. And I guess I am not sure if you are really enjoying playing the game anymore…"

Landlord: "I don't know…" or "Well, it is not always this bad…" or (smiling) "I'll just come to see you!"

You: "Let me ask you this: why did you get into the whole landlord – property owner thing in the first place? Was it for the cash flow? Was it to secure a better future? Maybe it's for the passive income?"

Landlord: "YES."

You: (smiling) "It's not a lot of fun right now, is it, and you're not making a lot of money if the tenants aren't paying. With all that I was thinking you might be open to a method where you can get back to where being a property owner was fun again. I'm talking about making everything a turnkey operation – you never have to collect rent, or do repairs, or screen tenants, or anything other than just collect a check each month. I mean, isn't that why you got into real estate in the first place?"

And if the landlord is interested?

At this point you can explain the lease option. ***Million Dollar Key***: <u>**It's a good idea to have the lease option forms available**</u>. Then you agree to finish off the eviction for free. And another deal goes into your portfolio.

Sometimes, you get people who aren't interested or, when you "pitch" them, they respond negatively. If that happens, you just backtrack like this.

You: "Okay, well what we need then is to get this eviction underway so you can go back to land lording!" (Note: contact them again in 6 months.)

And you help them with their eviction and pick up $200 bucks or so for your time. Easy enough. And that's the process. Easy enough? Here are some concerns:

How do you not practice law? *In the service agreement the landlord signs, there is a statement that says we are not giving legal advice*, rather the example forms we provide are merely that and if they are not sure of what they are doing they need to find legal representation. Also, it states your fee covers the education of the eviction process and the calendar we provide showing them what to do is only an example.

How do you know how to do an eviction? Well, if you are NOT an expert at this already, you should arrange to meet with an eviction attorney and pay him to answer everything. You can also contact a local investor's group go to www.REIA.com and see if there are eviction packets you can learn from.

How much do you charge, why do people use you and when do you collect? One expert charges $225. Why $225? Because the attorney in town does this for $475. The attorney in town is slow and files all of his documents weeks and weeks after he should. He is not a landlord and never has known the pain of eviction. He gets paid regardless of what he does. So the job of our example expert is to be better, cheaper and more effective. You collect your fee at the time you sign your agreement and start the forms.

Notes:

_____

_____

_____

_____

_____

_____

_____

_____

Chapter 5: Real Estate Investing Without Money

Does It Really Work?

Here are the case studies:

Most of us would like to acquire properties while taking as little money as possible out of our pocket. This allows us to have a reserve of security cash in the bank and allows us to use our money for other things such as investments, vacations and big-people toys.

You may be asking yourself how can a house be bought for less than 5-20% down plus <u>closing costs</u> and <u>pre-pays</u> (which typically amount to an additional $3,500). <u>The answer to your question is short and sweet – the lease purchase contract.</u>

These real-world examples will prove to you how quick and easy it is to buy a home with the lease purchase contract:

Experience #1:

While sitting at my desk shuffling through some paperwork, I got a phone call from a friend of mine who knew I was looking to move near his neighborhood. He told me that he drove by a beautiful home on a lake that had a For Rent sign in the front yard and that it would be perfect for me. So I drove by the home for myself to see what it was all about. It was perfect!

I jotted down the phone number from the sign and returned home. I did some research to determine what the home might be worth and what the fair market rent was. With my numbers in hand, I drove back out of the home and knocked on the door.

To my amazement, it was old friends who were clients of mine when I was selling insurance a few years ago. I couldn't believe it!

We talked about old times and, in short order, got down to business. They told me that they were asking $1,600 per month for rent. I asked them if they would consider selling their home and they said yes, as long as they got no less than $180,000. I knew from my research that their home was worth a little more.

I offered them the following lease purchase deal: $2,650 down (first month's rent, plus $1,000 for the option deposit), $1,650 per month rent, $300 per month rent credit, a term of 4 years and a sales price of $195,000. They accepted my offer without batting an eye.

The owners now have a positive monthly cash flow of $480, they have a tenant who will take care of their home as if it their own (which it is), they have a written sales agreement for $195,000 in 4 years plus they saved thousands of dollars in real estate commissions.

In 4 years I will have $20,200 in equity ($400 x 48 months + $1,000) so I probably won't have to come up with a down payment when we close, I paid a minimum amount of money to gain control of a wonderful home, my closing costs are delayed for 4 years, I will profit from any appreciation in value of this home, I don't pay any taxes and have limited exposure to liability. This entire process took less than two days to complete!

Notes:

_____

_____

_____

_____

_____

_____

_____

_____

Experience #2:

Isn't it great to know you can invest and make more money with fewer headaches using leverage to control homes, not own them?

Every real estate investor knows about leverage (the use of borrowed funds to improve one's capacity and to increase the rate of return on an investment). And every real estate investor does NOT know that if you control a home, rather than own it, you can make huge profits with very little expense.

What do I mean when I say "control homes?" What I mean is this… You have total and complete control over every single aspect of the home, but, your name is not on the deed. You can live in the home, you can make improvements to the home and you can even sell the home.

How is this possible? It is simple really. **A lease contract** puts you in immediate control of a home as far as **occupancy** is concerned. When you throw **an option to purchase contract** into the mix, you now have **an exclusive right to buy the home at a later specified time for a specific amount of money**.

Let's talk about how we can make a lot of money with very few headaches using leverage to control these homes. I will try to keep it short and sweet.

First, find a seller and negotiate the control of his/her home with a lease purchase contract. Let's say that Sally the seller agrees to lease purchase her home to you for the following terms: $700 per month rent, $1,700 down ($1,000 option deposit and $700 for first month's rent), a $250 monthly rent credit, a sales price of $75,000 and a term of 1 year. Assume that you got a pretty good deal and there is a little room for mark-up.

Since you know the value and appeal of the lease purchase contract to buyers who cannot qualify for a mortgage for one reason or another, you can jack up your sales price and monthly payment. You place a classified ad in your local newspaper and your phone rings off the hook. **Your ad reads like this,**
"Rent-to-Own. No Qualifying! $3,800 down, $800 per month."

You find an interested tenant/buyer and tell them your terms: $800 per month rent, $3,800 down ($3,000 option deposit and $800 for first month's rent), a $100 monthly rent credit, a sales price of $89,000 and a term of 1 year.

Your tenant/buyer likes your terms so you run <u>them through the pre-qualification process</u>. They are perfect so you close the deal.

<u>How much did you make? According to my profit calculation form, you will make exactly $2,100 up front, $100 in monthly rental payments and $13,800 in back end profit for a total net profit of $17,000 in one year.</u>

Let's take a step back for a moment and see what you've accomplished. You've gone out and controlled a home for 1 year for a total of $17,000. You got a good deal on the home and the only risk you were taking is that it might take you a couple weeks to find a qualified tenant/buyer. Well, I've got news for you...

When someone sees an advertisement for a lease purchase deal in the newspaper, they are all over it. Why? Because you are offering financing terms that no bank, mortgagor or lender can touch with a ten-foot pole.

Imagine doing four or five of these deals a year. I do one to two of these deals each month because they're quick, easy and lucrative!

But I've saved the best for last. If you didn't want the headaches associated with being a landlord, you could *<u>assign (sell)</u> your interest in your lease purchase agreement to a third party – maybe another real estate investor. But, it's still worth $5,000 per transaction (@ average). You could stick your up front profit of $2,100 in your pocket and sell your remaining interest for at least a couple thousand dollars! Now that's a great way to make some money in a hurry.

I received a lot of calls from sellers that weren't motivated, a few calls from other investors, but, fortunately for me, I did receive a call from a supremely motivated seller.

She said she was tired of renting to her deadbeat, lazy and unappreciative tenant, the tenant happened to be her son! He thought he was a real handyman and tried to remodel a few things. Ultimately, he broke everything he touched.

In early April, 2002 the seller and I negotiated a 1-year lease purchase with 2 (1) year extensions. I gave her $100 of option consideration and the contract began in May 2002. I agreed to pay her mortgage payments of $875 per month and I agreed to pay her mortgage balance at the beginning of each year. I received a copy of her loan statement and the right to notify her mortgage company that I should be contacted if there were any late payments.

I didn't do any repairs, or any clean up. I just placed a "handyman special" ad in the paper and received over 50 calls! Of the 50+ calls, only about 3 would take the property "as is." I settled on my buyer/tenant because she was a handy person, had lots of tools and was in the construction business. The tenant/buyer and I agreed that she'd pay me $1,050 in rent and I'd give her 50% rent credit toward the purchase price. I was excited and in a hurry and sheepishly asked for only $1,500 in option money. *(Mistake #1)*

Boy, did I make the wrong decision! I checked her credit and it sure was stinky. But, I thought, she's going to fix-up the place. Why not give her a break? *(Mistake #2)*

Next, she couldn't come up with the initial rent and option consideration without relying on a contractor that she had worked for. This method of paying me proved to be prevalent throughout the several months that followed. *(Mistake #3)*

Well, I was Ms. Forgiving and understanding and thought she'd get back on her feet real soon. **(Mistake #4)**

Of the 8 months she was in the property, she paid for 4 months rent and I paid the rest. Never once, was I late to the seller. The seller received my rent payment on or before the 5th of the month, even though the deadbeat tenant I carried on my back was always late and always had a sob story.

So November 2002's rent was late again and as usual I'm sweating and stressing, but, I'd had enough. I took the advice of a "I will not be continuously manipulated by tenants" fellow investor and started the eviction process. I hired a company that handled the entire process for me and, she was out by the 8th of December. The property looked almost exactly like it did before I rented to her, except now there was more crap in the yard. Man, was I downhearted!

I went back to the property to start to remove the stuff she left behind. I had also listed the property with the MLS service and started to get some bites. Well, when I checked to see if any prospective buyer/tenants had called, I hear a message from a caller who wanted to buy it and he wanted to know my price! I called him back, told him my price. I thought he'd want to rent it for a few months and start getting a few months of generous rent credit. Boy was I wrong and glad to be wrong. He said that he wanted me to stop all work and repairs; he had cash and wanted to buy the property right now! Hmmm where have I heard that before?

Even as dense and stressed as I was, I noticed a tone of urgency. So, I told him my price, which was $120,000. He agreed! He had an agent, but, she was supportive. I found out from the agent that the next-door neighbor and the buyer are best friends. They've been trying to live next to each other for years.

He took the property "as-is" with a contingency. I had to pay for a termite report. Well, that cost me $880 and it came out of escrow. Oh, the agent's fee came out of escrow, too. The buyer was true to his word and we sailed through escrow without a hitch. We closed several months ago and I received my check for $17,000. I actually thought the amount would be less.

A few more things… During this 8-month period, I resigned my position as a Director of community commercial lending to pursue real estate investing and wealth creation with friends and acquaintances with similar visions. After mentioning my experience to a few others, some wanted some of the action. So, I feel pretty good and look forward to spending my time and attention with Lease Purchase Investing.

Notes:

_____

_____

_____

_____

_____

_____

_____

Experience #3: It's been a while so let me update you on the deal I've got going. I found this cute little home in a nice neighborhood that was priced right ($60,000 – about $2,000 less than what I thought it was worth). Anyways, the seller wanted out of it so I made her a lease purchase and she accepted! My terms were: $1,000 option deposit, $550/mo for 24 months, $200 rent credit. I couldn't believe that she accepted my offer – it was like I bought this nice little home for a total of $1,550 down. Wow!

Before I signed the paperwork with her to close my deal, I ran two ads looking for tenants/ buyers. Much to my delight, my phone didn't stop ringing with interested people for three full days! I found a potential tenant/buyer and showed them the home and they wanted it. I had a sales price of $69,900 in 24 months (should have no problem appraising at this), received $2,000 down for the option money, charged $650/month and gave a $100 rent credit. Of course, I checked their credit and it wasn't perfect, but, they shouldn't have any problems getting a mortgage if they pay off a couple of late pays.

Notes:

_____

_____

_____

_____

_____

_____

Experience #4:

After just about giving up on calling the classified ads, I finally found one seller who was more than a little motivated and quickly set an appointment to meet with him. I explained to him, just how you teach, the features and benefits of lease purchasing his home. It worked like a charm! After several cups of coffee and a few firm handshakes, he decided that I could solve his real estate problems. The numbers looked like this:

My Purchase Price: $105,000
Option Deposit: $750
Monthly Rent: $795
Rent Credit: $100
Term: 1 year with 3 options to renew

I pulled some comps and talked to some Realtors so I know his home is worth around $112,000 – I can only speculate where property values are going to go, but, I have a pretty good idea. The beauty of the whole thing was that I already had a tenant/buyer lined up for this home – just like you said. Here is what their numbers looked like:

Their Purchase Price: $119,900
Option Deposit: $3,000
Monthly Rent: $875
Rent Credit: $100
Term: 1 year with 0 options to renew

Their credit was a little below par, but, they were only minor problems. I knew they'd be able to get a mortgage in a year – no problem.

When everything falls into place I will profit $2,250 up front, $960 in 12 monthly payments and my back end should be at least $10,000 after closing costs. As I sit here and think about this deal, I'm sure you can do at least one of these each month. And if only 65% of them closed, you'd still be making over $100,000 per year.

Notes:

_____

_____

_____

_____

_____

_____

_____

Once You Have Control of a House, What's the Best Way to Move It?

If an investor wants to sell a house to generate capital for the business, the quicker the sale, the more money the investor can make on the deal. Waiting for the house to sell creates expenses that erode away the potential profits.

Therefore, our sales strategy is designed to appeal to the largest possible market. *The biggest group of homebuyers in any community is the first-time buyers. New stimulus funding has made this an even larger marketplace as first-time homebuyers qualify for an $8,000 tax credit (based on an itemized tax return).* There are others who are moving in from out of town, are moving up because they have more money, need a bigger place because they have more kids. Even many of those coming in from out of town will be looking for starter homes because they can't afford more.

This being the case, we want to work out a strategy for appealing to people in this group and techniques for getting their attention quickly and helping them move through the process quickly. The latter consideration is important because, as first time buyers, they have never gone through the process before and is likely to be scary and foreign to them. That means that the service we render in helping them along will be rewarded on top of the rewards we gain for selling the house.

First Time Homebuyers?

It is good to remember the feelings and perspectives of the members of our target market. People buy according to their feelings. Here is something to remember about them:

- ➤ They don't always know how to proceed.
- ➤ Many don't expect to be able to buy a house anytime soon because they don't believe they can afford one.
- ➤ Some grew up in a renter's environment (their family always rented) and they believe that is their lot in life, as well.
- ➤ It is easy for these people to see themselves on the fringes of society, on the outside looking in.
- ➤ Feeling excluded, many of them mistrust institutions, such as banks, government and real estate companies.

The monthly payment on an FHA loan will be very much the same as these are already paying in rent, but, you can point out that it will not increase on a landlord's whim and they get a tax write-off on the interest. *Furthermore, you will help them get the funds for the down payment, so that needn't be a concern.*

Advertising That Doesn't Cost Much

Since our target market doesn't expect to buy a house soon, they will not be looking for realtor signs. Since they do rent, however, they will notice the hand-made signs you put up. For signboard, we suggest you get tile board from Home Depot and cut it down to size. One 4' x 8' sheet will give you 8 signs that are 2 foot square. You can write on the sign with a felt-tip marker. Your cost per sign will be approximately $1.50. Here is an example wording of a suggested sign. We will explain each element below:

HOME FOR SALE
RENT TO OWN
$700 DEPOSIT
CALL 555-9876

The sign does not give an address. **You can re-use this sign for different deals.** If you put it up on public property (parking strips along city streets, etc., do so on a Friday afternoon and then pick them up again early Monday morning, so that city employees don't take them down. Even better get permission from friends to put them up on private property. They only need be in the same part of town as the house.

Here is an explanation of the sign:

➢ We call attention to the sale portion of the transaction with the first line.
➢ We put **"Rent to Own" in larger letters**, because this is the grabber. Most people who are renting now would love to buy a home, but, don't feel like they can right now. Reading this, they are likely to think, "Oh, I'm already renting, so I can do that, but, now I can do what I've been doing all along and still own a place!"
➢ The amount of the deposit is equal to whatever you would charge for rent on this house, were you to rent it out. That makes it equivalent to what your potential buyers are used to paying for a security deposit on their lease, which they feel they can handle.
➢ *Make sure that you have voice mail on this phone line, since you can't always be there to answer.* Voice mail is better than a machine, because it can pick up while you are talking on the phone and you don't miss any calls.

With a monthly payment the same as they are used to, with the advantage that it won't go up with inflation and no worries about the down payment, why would any of these people not want to purchase your home? In fact, what you are selling here is not the house, per se*; it is the concept of affordable home-ownership.* Which house it may be is almost secondary. The sale is made on the excitement of this couple being able to buy a house of their own! Because of the other realities above, we approach the market as just regular people, not slick professionals. Our advertising is homemade; our approach is low-keyed and simple.

The plan comes in five steps, which can begin as soon as the investor signs a contract for purchase of a suitable house. In fact, all purchase contracts should contain a clause in the addendum allowing immediate access to the house for the purchase of showing it to potential occupants. With luck and some work, your buyers could close on their purchase simultaneous with your purchase of the house, meaning very low costs on your acquisition and more profit into your pocket. Here are the five steps:

Step One: Put up a dozen signs around the neighborhood. You could put the same message on fliers and distribute them to the public via bulleting boards in town. This keeps your cost down.
Step Two: As you talk to the callers responding to your signs and fliers, you want to

accomplish two tasks:

➤ Make sure this house is suitable to the caller. If the caller has 6 kids and the house has two bedrooms, it won't do much good to pursue things. However, now you have a contact that would likely be interested in any 4-bedroom house you can supply. Get information and go find a house for these people; you will know how you are disposing of it before you even sign the purchase agreement.

➤ Gather the information you will need to get **the caller pre-qualified for FHA financing**. *Check with your mortgage professional.* Don't pump the caller for lots of information or you will lose them. Remember that they may mistrust institutions and now you are acting just like a banker if you ask too many questions.

➤ Submit the information to mortgage professional, which will provide a pre-approval in approximately 72 hours or less. If yes, get in contact with the caller again and set a time to meet at the house together. *This will be the first time the caller even knows the address.*

Step Three: Meet with the potential buyers at the house and let them look at it. The emphasis of your conversation should be on the exciting concept that they can own their own home. Also let them talk about what colors they would choose for paint and flooring. Let them dream. As quickly as possible, ideally at the time of the first visit, you would like to accomplish the following:

➤ Have the buyer sign the sell and buy agreement and give you the deposit called for on the sign. *This deposit will go into an escrow account maintained by whoever will do your closing (either a title company or an attorney depending on the State the property is located).*

➤ Have the buyer fill out the FHA loan application packet. This packet has as many as 18 pages and call for several signatures per applicant, along with a half dozen places for applicant's initials. Without some help and guidance, your clients will likely undergo a panic attack. *At the time you set up this meeting, you should have notified the mortgage expert to be on call.* He or she also has several other people sent by you to place loans for, because you only have one house to sell and several people were interested. The mortgage person should be willing to get the application filled out here and now even if over the phone. It is wise to strike while the iron is hot, while the buyers feel the enthusiasm and euphoria of obtaining their own home. If the mortgage person can't make it, you will have to be the one to hold the buyers' hands. **By no means should you simply hand them the packet and say, "go home and fill this out and bring it back to me**. You will never see them again.

Step Four: After a period of time, you will hear from the mortgage broker than the loan has been approved. That means that it is time to take two more steps.

➤ *Have the buyers sign a lease and move into the house*. They will be ecstatic and you will collect an occupancy deposit in approximately the same amount as the first deposit. It, too, goes into escrow. The lease should be open-ended, because it is not yet certain how long they will rent the house from you. It depends on how much down payment money they need.

> ➤ ***Get a statement from an FHA appraiser about the dollar value of sweat equity work that your buyers can perform.*** Anybody can paint and every house you buy should be painted inside. FHA will recognize the going rate for the job in that community. For painting the interior of a 1,100 square foot house this is generally around $800. If the work to be done requires licensing in your community, the person doing the work must be licensed. This would include things such as electrical or plumbing work. If the buyer is licensed, that provides a great opportunity. The work can also be performed by relatives and gifted to the buyers. You get to pay for all materials, but, your buyers are credited for the work toward their down payment.

Step Five: When work is done and carpet is laid, you get a final "as is" appraisal and schedule the closing. On homes priced below $80,000, it is likely that the deposits and sweat equity have covered the 3% down payment required. If the home is higher priced and all the work to be done is the interior painting, the buyers will have to come up with more. FHA allows a number of means outside of personal savings:

> ➤ Money can be lent to the buyers by a relative (but not by the seller, or any other person taking part in the transaction, such as a real estate agent, mortgage broker, etc.)
> ➤ Money can be gifted to the buyers by a relative.
> ➤ Sweat equity.
> ➤ The buyer can tender a surplus of rent paid; this means that if the lease calls for an amount at the low end of the range of rents recognized for this type of house in this neighborhood, but, the tenant pays the high end of the rent and this goes through the escrow account, from which the rent due you is paid. Then the surplus paid accumulates toward the down payment. In a few months, there will be enough there along with sweat equity credits to close the deal.

The end result is that anybody who can qualify for FHA financing can buy your starter home with a month or so. If they cannot qualify for reasons of credit history, their possible recourse is to enter into a lease option agreement with you. ***Two years of good payments will clear up nearly any credit problem and in two years, they can now finance the house.***

Using these techniques, it is possible to sell a modest home very quickly, with a selection of interested buyers. The quicker you sell the more money you make. Whether or not you let your realtor in on the process is up to you. If you have a true companion, enrolled in the All-Star System, you certainly should. If you don't have strong feelings for an agent, you could do this yourself and save an additional 4%-6%.

That's money in the bank!

Details You Need to Know

Just in case you might be worried that the tenant might not exercise their option in the term agreed, just remember that *80% **do not.*** So what do you do? You turn around and offer it to someone else with a consideration up front, only now adjust the monthly amount to reflect current market conditions and increase the purchase price according to current market conditions and sit back and let it generate more income for you.

What a deal!

Notes:

_____

_____

_____

_____

_____

_____

_____

_____

_____

_____

_____

_____

_____

_____

_____

_____

_____

_____

Chapter 6: What to do 1st and Where Do I Begin?

As Stephen Covey tells us *(The Seven Habits of Highly Effective People)*, you should **begin with the end in mind**. You want to know what to do after you find a motivated seller with a house you can buy well below market. If you find the house first then try to figure out what to do with it, you might inherit a nightmare. Certain preparation ensures a good and profitable experience, beginning with lining up your real estate investment team.

> ➤ **Rehab investors or Retailers to buy your contract.**
> ➤ **A title company or an attorney to close the (Know how it works in your state).**
> ➤ **Most important – a good contract or agreement.**

Let's go over each of these in a little more detail.

How To Find Investors That Will Buy Your Contract

For a moment, imagine yourself as a Retailer, with the capital you need to buy a house to fix up and sell again. You enjoy the work – maybe you're a handy man, or maybe you just enjoy the profits from a good sale. Most likely, you would rather let someone else do the footwork for you.

Your job as a Finder or a Dealer is to find deals for the Retailers. But first locate the Retailers so you know where to turn when you have a hot prospect. They're not trying to hide out, so you only need know where to look:

1. Daily Things To Do

> ➤ **Read Newspaper Ads.** Look in the daily and weekly newspapers for the "We Buy Houses" ads.
> ➤ You may even find billboards or signs around town that say, "We Buy Houses."
> ➤ **Participate in locate Real Estate Investor Association (REIA) or www.reia.com .** Not only are *these groups good educational experiences, but, also you meet and mingle with a host of people who are happy to give you money for properties, or even participate with you in the acquisition of other properties*. Most major metropolitan areas have at least one club that meets monthly. <u>You need to join and attend every meeting.</u> **The networking (collect their information and give them yours) opportunities are endless**. When you go to the meetings tell everyone what you are planning to do. **Once again, collect names and information about people who are interested in buying houses**.

Attend real estate auctions, not as a participant, but, to meet the investors that gather. Foreclosure auctions and tax sales take place on a county basis, but, don't forget estate sales. Some investors hate to go out knocking on doors and dealing with emotional, distressed owners; they much prefer to buy at the foreclosure auction. At most auctions, the property must be paid for with cash or cashier's check within hours of the sale. *What a wonderful opportunity for you to meet cash buyers for the houses you find.*

Introduce yourself to the investors and hand out business cards. Tell them you find houses just like the ones sold at the auction and ask if they would be interested in being contacted when you find something. Just as you did with the "We Buy Houses" ads, you need to find out where and what price range they buy in. Ask for their business card and make notes on the back or take along notebook. Make sure and do this either before or after the auction because the investors will be focused on bidding during the auction and won't appreciate distractions.

Notes:

_____

_____

2. Keeping Things Organized

Keep an information sheet or data base on each investor you meet.

Be honest and tell them that you are just starting out and will be looking for houses that need to be rehabbed. Make sure you find out what locations they prefer and the price range they look to. Some are particular about these things, and others will accept any good deal from any location. Find out if they are a cash buyer or if they will need some extra time to arrange financing.

Keep Telephone Logs

Once word gets around that you flip contracts, you may get weekly phone calls from investors asking if you have anything. Keep a log of who calls; these will be the first investors you need to contact when you have a deal.

3. How To Find A Good Title Company Or/And Attorney

A good reason for **networking with other investors** is to find out whom they use for these tasks. By building a good relationship with the investors you call from ads, meet at the investor clubs or at the auction, you'll develop a base of mentors that you can call anytime you need advice. Don't abuse the privilege though. Rarely will you make friends with someone if you call them frequently and keep them on the phone for a long time. Keep your phone calls brief and to the point. Usually if you find one, you have found them both.

Or better yet, take advantage of the time at the investor club meetings for your questions. **Some investor clubs even arrange for legal counsel for members for a low fee or include it as a perk of membership.**

4. The Agreement or Contract

Finding the motivated seller with the right house and the right price is the starting point. Now you need to tie it up. You need a document that gives you control over the property so that you are able to make money from it. A rule of real estate tells us that if it's not in writing, it doesn't exist. Here you can record all the points that you and the seller have agreed to orally. A contract lets the seller know you're serious about buying their house and it provides written instructions for the title company. All real estate contracts must be in writing.

There are a number of good sources for such a contract. That means there is no reason to wing it. Your best bet is to consult with an attorney to have your contract written in your best interest. If you don't have the funds to pay an attorney, the next best thing would be to start with your state's real estate commission contract then add, or subtract, a few key clauses. **A contract from an office supply store will be too vague**. Don't take that chance. The contracts used by a Realtor or that you can get from a title company will work well too. Finally, your local real estate investor club may have a good contract for you to use.

Whichever agreement or contract you use be sure to add a clause that protects YOUR interest and allows you a way out of the contract. Examples are:

Subject to approval of Buyer's partner."

> Note: Many real estate agents are wise to this one and recognize it as an escape clause. If they question you on this, simply explain, "This is a silent partner who wishes to remain anonymous."

"This agreement is subject to Buyer's approval of satisfactory building Inspection within 15 days."

"This contract may be assigned; in such event, the buyer named herein is Released of all further liability"

"This offer is contingent upon buyer obtaining new financing of their choice of $140,000 at 8% per annum over 30 years."

> These are simply a few examples. You would use the numbers that pertain to this particular deal, with an interest rate close to the prevailing purchase-money mortgage rate www. bankrate.com . Then if the rate you get is higher (which it probably will be, since this is investment financing), you have the choice of withdrawing from the deal or waiving this clause.

If you cannot find a buyer for the contract, you notify the Seller in writing that your partner did not approve the purchase of the house, or that you did not get the specified financing. Then you are no longer obligated to purchase the property. **You should send the notice by _certified mai (return receipt requested)._**

Everything you and the Seller agree to must be written in the contract or agreement. If it's not, the Seller may develop a sudden case of amnesia. If the property is vacant, you can add the following clauses to the contract:

"Buyer to receive access to property upon acceptance of contract for the purpose of making repairs or showing the property to prospective tenants."

If the house you are buying is listed with a realtor, any real estate agent can get you in to show it and your team agents should be happy to do so. If, however, the property is not listed, instead is for sale by owner, then you need a more reliable access. What if the seller suddenly goes on a 3-week fishing trip to Iceland? In this case you need your own key so you can get in whenever it suits you. Add the following to the first statement, and you are covered:

"Buyer to receive keys to property upon acceptance of this agreement."

You may even ask the Seller to allow you to place a For Sale or For Rent sign in the yard prior to closing. Whatever you agree to, put it in the contract.

It is essential that the contract does **<u>NOT</u>** have any clauses that would prevent you from assigning the contract.

Notes:

_____

_____

_____

_____

_____

_____

_____

_____

_____

Chapter 7: How To Find Houses For Assignment / Motivated Sellers

Before going on, let's review the preliminary steps to complete before you actually close a contract for purchase on a house you plan to flip.

> ➢ **Locate three or more rehab investors to flip contracts to.**
> ➢ **Have your contracts ready and thoroughly understand them.**
> ➢ **Know which title-company or attorney you will use to close that first flip deal.**

Now let's discuss how you can increase your odds of finding and closing more deals in the least amount of time. *Here are four ways to find houses:*

1. **Farming for Houses**
2. **Tell the World – Recruit Bird Dogs (see chapter 12)**
3. **Research, Research, Research**
4. **Advertising (free or low budget guerilla marketing mostly available online)**

A combination of all four gives you the best results and greatest success. However, you may have other time constraints (maybe a full-time job) that limit what you can do. In that case, **pick the methods that best fit your schedule or your budget.**

1. Farming For Houses – www.fsbo.com or www.forsalebyowners.com

Your best farm area would comprise a 10 to 15 mile radius of your home. If you live in a major metropolitan area, it wastes time and money to drive all over town to look for houses. You'll quickly find that you are spending more time driving than actually looking at houses or talking to motivated sellers.

Get to know your farm area like you know the back of your hand. It's not hard to do: working just a few hours on the weekends will teach you a lot. Drive around within each neighborhood in your farm area. **Keep a log or journal with information about your target neighborhoods**. The best neighborhoods for flipping have houses that are about 20 years old. Newer houses probably won't have enough equity to allow for a profitable deal.

Find the for sale signs in these neighborhoods. Write down the address and contact numbers in your log then call to find out the square footage, number of bedrooms and baths, how long it's been on the market and what's the asking price. Keep all this information in your log. With this information you have just established the approximate market value of houses in the neighborhood.

If all the houses are newer or in good condition then you simple need to find a different farm area.

What To Look For

Vacant houses: How do you spot a vacant house? Tall grass is certainly a give away, as is a porch or doorway cluttered with phone books, flyers and coupons from the local pizza parlor. Or perhaps a mailbox stuffed with mail that has not been picked up. Boarded up windows are a sure sign of a vacant house.

When you find a vacant house, check with the neighbors to *find out who owns the house*. You want to find out how long they lived there, why they moved, how you can reach them, how long has it been vacant – in other word, get any information you can about the owner and the house.

Let the neighbors know that you are looking for houses to buy in the neighborhood and that you work with a group of investors (these are your "partners") that will remodel the house then sell it to a good homeowner. Chances are they are very anxious to have a "good" neighbor and will cooperate. Don't forget to ask if they know of any other houses that are vacant or in need of repair in the neighborhood. If you leave your business card, they may think of a house after you leave and you want to make sure they know how to get in touch with you.

Sometimes the neighbors just won't give you names and numbers of the owner. If that happens, leave your business card and ask them to please get a message to the owner that you are interested in buying the house.

Your next step is to *check the property tax records*. The names of your fellow taxpayers is public information and therefore available to you. Most property taxes are paid on a county level, so this is the place to start. Some tax offices will give you the owner's name and address with just a phone call, others require that you come in to check it yourself. Many Counties' tax records are on the Internet example for New York www.nyc.org/finance . This is the first place to investigate.

Once you find out who the owner is you can either ***send them a letter or postcard*** or try to get their phone number and call them. *Directory assistance may well have it, or **Internet white pages** (inclusive of the reverse search mechanism)* may work. Let the owner know you saw their house at that particular address and may be interested in buying it. Ask if they are interested in selling and get as many details about the house as possible.

Some things you need to find out are:

1. How many bedrooms, bathrooms, garages – what is the approximate square footage? How old is the house? Does it have central heat and air? Why did they move? (These questions are just to warm them up for the important questions).
2. Is there a mortgage on the house? If so, what is the approximate payoff?
3. Are there any liens or judgments against the property?
4. What repairs need to be done? Estimated costs?
5. How long have they owned the house?

From this information you can decide if the house is a good flip candidate or if you should just mark it off your list. For example:

If they tell you they owe $40,000 on the mortgage and the house needs extensive repairs including foundation work, but, you know from the information in your log that homes in good condition in the neighborhood are selling for $55,000. You can quickly determine from this information that this house just won't work.

They tell you they lived in the house for 30 years and the mortgage is paid off but it needs $10,000 in repairs and they just don't have the money for repairs? You know from the information in your log that homes in good condition are selling for $55,000. This has all the ingredients of a potential deal; lots of equity, a motivated seller and a house that needs work.

They tell you they owned the house for one year but just couldn't keep up with the payments. Because it's such a new mortgage you can determine that they probably owe about what the house is worth and it's not a flip candidate.

You are looking for houses with at least 40 percent equity – the more the better! So if houses in good condition are selling for $60,000, you want to find houses that have at least $20,000 in equity.

A real winning combination is a house with plenty of equity that needs repairs. Often is the excessive repairs that motivate a seller to sell below market; they think it will take $20,000 to fix the house and they don't have the money and have no way to ever get the money. In reality it will cost less.

Occupied houses in need of repair: Sometimes the first sign of a motivated seller is a house that screams "PLEASE HELP ME" when you drive by. Perhaps the owner is having financial difficulty and just can't afford to maintain the house. Or perhaps that's just the way they live. Maybe it's a rental and the landlord won't put any money into fixing the house.

You'll never know which situation it is until you contact the homeowner. To do this, you can:

1. Knock on the door and tell the occupant you are looking for houses to buy in the neighborhood and ask if they would be interested in selling (or know someone who is). Make sure to leave a business card. If it's a renter, try to get the owner's name and number.

2. Write down the address, look up the owner in the tax records and send a letter or postcard saying you are looking for houses to buy in the neighborhood and want to know if they would be interested in selling (or know someone who is).

3. Look up the owner in the tax records, find out their phone number then call with the same information as #2.

If you send a letter or postcard, you may not get a response the first time. Continue mailing to them every three to four weeks.

When you knock on the door they may say they aren't interested in selling right now. That can change as they think about it. Follow up with a letter or postcard every three or four weeks. Stop by the house occasionally to remind them that you are still interested in buying.

An alternative to the postcard might be to leave a flyer on their door (and all the other doors in the neighborhood) with the message: "I Buy Houses – Cash – Quick Close – Any Condition.

If they show some interest in selling, then you need to ask the questions listed above to see if it is a candidate for a flip.

The follow-up is VERY important. Time has a way of changing everything – even turning an unmotivated seller into a motivated seller.

2. Tell the World – Recruit Bird Dogs: Use forms in Chapter 12 only after due diligence

You can expand your farm area and not take up any more of your valuable time by telling everyone you come in contact with that you are looking for run-down houses to buy. Tell all your co-workers, the people at the grocery store, everyone at church, your kid's friend's parents, your kid's teachers, the guy that fixes your car, the people at the cleaners, the waitress at Denny's, the people at the barber shop or beauty shop, etc., etc. The more eyes and ears you have out there looking for you, the more deals you will do.

You will find that it can be fun to network with bird dogs. As an example, from now on, you should never pay for gasoline at the pump. Gas pumps can't give you referrals, but, the attendant in the convenience store certainly can. The fun part comes when you discover the secret that makes everyone you meet want and love to talk to you.

Here's the secret. Ask yourself, what topic are people universally most interested in talking about anytime anywhere? The answer. Themselves.

If you have the attention of the convenience store clerk for 30 seconds while he or she swipes your credit card, or of the pizza delivery guy while you write out a check, you grab his or her attention immediately if whatever you talk about is from his or her perspective. If the subject is the weather, let it be the weather as they see it, or as it affects them. If it is the price of rice in China, let them tell you how they feel about it, or what they know about it. Maybe you have a Ph.D. in Asian rice economics, but, if you let the plumber tell you about how it all works, he'll think you're a top-notch human being and will be happy to give you 30 seconds to explain that you buy houses and would like him to find some for you.

<u>Always give your bird dog a number of business cards</u>. The business card lets everyone know you are serious and it insures they have a way to contact you when they find a house. Tell them to write their own name and how you get in contact with them on the back of the card. Why? You let them know you ***<u>pay a finder's fee of $250 to $500 or more for each house that CLOSES</u>***.

Real-Life Example:

"The very first flip deal I did was because I told my best friend's mother that I was going to get into the real estate business. I told her I was looking for houses to buy that were run down and I'd pay a finder's fee to anyone that found houses for me.

A few days later she just happened to overhear someone where she works talking about a house he inherited from his mother. It had been a rental and was so run down that he thought it could not be sold. She told him I was looking for run down houses to buy. A few weeks later he had his house sold, a rehabber had a new project, my "bird dog" had $500 and I had a check for $4,000.

Finally, take the time to get to know the mail carriers, newspaper carriers, UPS drivers and Fed Ex drivers assigned to your farm area as well as people that do lawn work. These people travel all over town and can help to expand your farm area. Make sure everyone you talk to have your business card and know what you are looking for and know you pay a finder's fee for any houses you are able to buy.

3. Research, Research, Research

Often a recent event creates a motivated seller. We have listed some of these events below. Many of these events, like a foreclosure, are time sensitive – meaning you have a window of opportunity to act and after a certain date it is too late to buy the house from the owner. It is good to find out what the state laws are concerning these "events" so you'll know how much time you have. You can get information about all these properties at your county courthouse, tax office or other city municipal offices.

Also you may also have a legal newspaper where this information is posted daily or weekly.

> - **Foreclosure – Trustee sales**
> - **Foreclosure – Tax sales**
> - **Code Violations (red tags)**
> - **Divorce**
> - **Probate – death of owner**
> - **Evictions – landlords with bad tenant**
> - **Bankruptcy (Chapter 7 liquidation)**
> - **Criminal Act – going to jail**
> - **Out of State Owner**
> - **Liens or Judgments**

Although these properties may take you outside your farm area, you know that the seller is likely to be highly motivated, which increases your odds of getting a great deal. Since you are researching this at the courthouse, you can also check up on the probability of equity while you are at the courthouse before you even contact the owners. Why waste time pursuing a deal with no equity?

How can you determine there is enough equity? First, find out when the deed was recorded. The longer the owner has owned the house, the more equity they will have in the house. If the deed was recorded 2 years ago, you can scratch that lead off your list. On the other hand, if the deed date is 10 or 15 years old or more jump on that one right away. As a rule of thumb, you can figure that a 10 year-old deed equals 40% equity or higher.

Of course, if you don't have time (or lack the inclination) to research these properties, you can *hire someone to do the research for you*. However, you will need to train them how, so you better learn how first. Some County Courthouses offer free classes to teach you how to research properties.

Find out if they do in your area and take the time to learn. Otherwise, just let one of the employees show you how. Government bureaucrats don't receive incentives from their employer to provide excellent customer service, but, they do appreciate good, positive recognition. Let them know you admire their expertise and appreciate their service, and they will be more inclined to show you how to do your research.

You'll also need a good system for gathering information. This may as well be as sophisticated as a *laptop computer database* or as simple as a form you develop for entering the necessary information about the house and the owners. Keep it consistent for quick reference on any property or owner.

4. Advertising www.craigslist.org www.twitter.com www.facebook.com

Check the real estate section of your local newspapers for offline sources or the above referenced sites for online marketing sources. Most of the houses for sale in the newspaper are in good condition and the owners want top dollar. Besides, only a portion of the homes for sale shows up here at any one time because of the expense of classified ads.

However, sometimes you can find an ad with phrases like "Handyman Special," "Selling As Is," "Fixer Upper," "must sell ASAP," or "Estate Sale." We call these "motivation words" because they signal a motivated seller. Others would be "will consider any offer," "needs TLC," seller transferred.

Learn to skim through the ads and scan for these words. You may want to hold a hi-liter in your hand. Simply dot the words as you scan them, then go back and read only those ads with a dot of color. This spares you the time waste of reading ads for luxury homes on a lakefront with 2 wooded acres that are definitely candidates for flipping.

Consider running your own ad in the "Real Estate Wanted" section of the newspaper. If it's too expensive in the daily newspaper, check prices in the weekly newspaper like Green sheet or Thrifty Nickel. The more people that know you're looking for houses to buy, the more deals you'll do. Your ad could say, "We Buy Houses – CASH – Any Condition."

The fact of the matter is that there are a wide variety of activities that help you find deals. Brainstorm, think about it, and you may come up with something no one has ever thought of before. The key is your consistency and perseverance. It's a numbers game, and if you look at enough places, you will find enough deals to make you wealthy.

Let's Take A Quick Break Here

Now know the basics of how to put together contract flips. We still need to go over lease options, as well. But before we start, it might be good to look at one of the characteristics of a success real estate entrepreneur that will serve you well as you start your business.

Ancient wisdom tells us that we should be before we do, and do before we have. The opposite would say that we have to have all the trappings of an investor (the Cadillac, El Dorado, the double-breasted pin-striped suit, the fat cigar, the gold money clip, etc.) before you can do what investors do, and that until you do what investors do, you can't be one.

The truth is if you think like an investor, you will act like an investor and the having what investors have will take care of it.

Let's take a little time to check out what an investor really is. What follows are a collection of attitudes, thinking-processes and activities engages in by one particular and successful real estate investor. We asked this particular person how he finds the deals.

Q: You have achieved a great deal of consistency in your business. Has that been difficult for you?

A: Consistently putting deals together is easier than you think. Really! Making things happen and making serious money as a real estate investor doesn't require luck or extraordinary negotiation skills and it doesn't take talent or money or a master's degree in business.

None of that stuff matters. What does it take? In a word, **PERSISTENCE.**

I'm able to put deals together today because I *continually* get my message out to people who are looking for someone to help them out of their difficult situation.

Q: So you're saying that you keep at doing what works, you're successful?

A: Persistence Is The Key. You've heard of the "motivated seller"? Guess what happens when he's introduced to Mr. Motivated Buyer. I'll tell you what happens, deals! Things get signed off and someone ultimately writes a check with my name on it. And that's what it's all about.

Make sense? In order to put deals together consistently, just put your message into the hands of the people who are eager to sell and your success is virtually guaranteed. But you have to get your message out there consistently. Persistence is the key.

Q: What kinds of things do you do consistently?

A: There are lots of ways to pull it off. *I like postcards and I send them out by the hundreds every week*. Postcards deliver my six-line message with my phone number right there at the bottom and if someone is thinking about getting rid of his property about the same time that thing shows up I their mailbox, boom, there's a deal in the works.

But you can't just go send postcards to everyone. You need to target your mailing to the people who will most likely be looking for someone like you.

Example? We're always researching public records and pulling names and addresses of people in trouble and that includes people who are delinquent in the payment of their property taxes. After years of unpaid property taxes in this state, that property gets scheduled for a foreclosure auction. You think those folks might be motivated? You bet they are. We mailed out a bunch last week and I've got four or five calls to return on my voice mail right now.

Doing nothing more than this sort of thin, we consistently close six, eight or even a dozen deals virtually every month. Again, it's not luck or talent or skill that allows this to happen, it's getting that phone to ring with a hot-to-go seller on the other end.

There are people who right now, at this very moment, are hoping and praying for someone like you to appear in their lives and help them out of their mind. Heck, they could be right next-door. Now, ask yourself this: how would they find me?

Often, your only real answer is "they can't."

However, if that motivated seller is in my town, he can pick up the newspaper and see my ad, or call me on my signs or find us on our Internet sites or even – respond to our postcards. Because if he's in foreclosure, or going through an eviction, or is delinquent in his property taxes, or has an IRS lien, or hasn't paid his water bill, he's heard from me.

Q: What do you put on your postcards?

A: It's very simple, because I can't depend on everyone liking to read a lot. In fact, that's why we use postcards instead of letters. If you get a pile of mail and one of the envelopes has a mailing label on it, do you bother to open it? *Probably not.* Even though my postcard is obviously junk mail, you can't help but read the message. It's short, it's in big print and it jumps right out at you.

The message is simply that an investor is **looking for houses to buy, any condition , default or foreclosure situations OK,** pay cash, then my phone number. I make the print big enough to fill up most of the card. Some people even make the card a bright color so it stands out. If I find out from public records that a homeowner is in default on the mortgage, they might get my *postcard once a week*, because how else are they going to get out of trouble?

Q: So all you do to contact potential sellers is send postcards?

A: There Are Many Ways To Find Motivated Sellers. There are dozens of other paths to the motivated seller's door and spent figuring out who those folks might be is generally time well spent indeed. I specialize in systematically finding and targeting these motivated sellers.

We had a seller sell us a $35,000 property last month for $3,500, a Tenth of its value, because he could no longer even think about "that damn tenant" in the place. Now he responded to a postcard sent to delinquent property tax owners. But it works just as well with newspaper ads.

A seller paid me $500 yesterday to take over payments on his home. But he owed less than 80% of what it was worth and has an 8% loan with payments that will allow us positive cash flow. Reason for selling? The Air Force transferred him and unless he sold right now, his wife would have to stay behind until the house is sold. *He responded to my ad in the paper.*

Q: Is the text of your newspaper ad similar to the card?

A: It's pretty much the same. The nice thing is that the ad goes out to so many people for one cost. But it's not like the postcards are hugely expensive. It only costs 28 cents (as of the current time so check www.usps.gov for more information or your local post office) a piece to mail them and I print them off on my computer, four to a page on cardstock.

I get results from both ads and postcards. Oh, but, here's something that the postcard can do that ads don't. It's easier to hit out-of-state owners. Absentee owners are good to work with. The hassle of being in a different state provides its own motivation. Earlier this year, we bought three houses in one month on a mailing to out-of-state homeowners. In each instance, my postcard showed up in their mailbox at just the right time in their lives and they were sufficiently motivated to get that property out of their lives once and for all. Hey, good thing I showed up, because when the dust settles, we'll have netted over a hundred thousand dollars on these three deals alone. Get the idea?

Q: Bottom line, what you're doing seems to work?

A: I talked yesterday with at least six sellers who were responding to any one of my marketing strategies. **Six!** Now, not a one of them seems to have anything I'm likely to buy, but, that's not the point. The point is, people are calling.

Q: So now we're back where we started, with persistence.

A: Again, ask yourself: "How many sellers called me yesterday?" If the answer is "zip," then you've got some work to do. **<u>Lay the groundwork by getting your marketing in place</u>**. You don't need to do it all at once or have a dozen things in place for now. Just get yourself set up with at least one good marketing strategy that puts callers on the line.

***<u>If you can figure out a way to do that consistently, you're in business</u>*!!!**

Chapter 8: 30-DAY PLAN OF ACTION: (Using our 20 Step Process)

FOR A NEW REAL ESTATE INVESTOR

1. Solidify your plan.

Knowing with great clarity exactly what you want will take you a long way toward getting it. Start your plan with a powerful vision of what you desire your life to be, then create an effective mission statement to explain how you will get to that desired life-state, which will serve as an anchor for future goals. Decide with clarity what you want to accomplish over the next year, five years, and 10 years.

- What kinds of properties do you want to look for?
- How much time to you wish to spend each week?
  - ➢ You need to plan your calendar a week at a time. Set aside specific blocks of time each day for your business and don't allow anything to interfere.
  - ➢ Review your vision at least weekly, your mission statement daily and specific goals several times a day.

In case it's not clear what vision and mission statements are, there is more to come on this below.

2. Link up with a money source or better yet, a number of possible money sources.

The sections below on Mortgage Experts and on Money Partners provide background on how to do this. You should continually increase your network by marketing yourself at all times – the clerk at the 7-Eleven might have an uncle with enough money to fund your project.

3. Work at least 5-8 hours a week on real estate investing strategies.

Clearly the amount of time you put into your business pays dividends on your success. However, you have other demands on your time besides real estate investing and you have developed habits over the years that respond to these demands and don't welcome change in the routine.

Only careful planning will enable you to get done what this business requires for success. Some events in our life are urgent, others are unimportant. The two don't necessarily mean the same thing. Some events are urgent because they shout at you, but, have no importance at all (the loudly ringing telephone might be a wrong number). The quiet important things will become overwhelmed by the urgencies, whether important or not, if you don't plan for them.

Plan your business at least a week at a time.

Daily planning without weekly orientation becomes crisis management and you become subject to last minute urgencies that don't fit your mission statement.

Obviously, a major part of your planning will include your goals, particularly the short-term items that bring you to the long-term results. Be wise in your goal setting. It's important to not only have results goals but also performance goals (road map goals). Setting a goal to earn $10,000 a month within a year is great, but, your goals *__must__* also lay out how you will get there.

A sample plan might be:
a. **Talk to 20 sellers a week.**
b. **Visit and walk through 5 houses a week.**
c. **Make 2 offers a week.**
d. **Purchase one property a month.**
e. **One property = $10,000 / month.**

Based on these performance goals, you will be able to plan your income because each of these activities will produce a result that you can measure. Over a short period you will know how many calls you need to make and how many houses to visit and how many offers you must make to purchase one property that meets your purchase criteria.

4. Recruit real estate agents who will seek out deals for you and provide comps.

This is definitely worth discussing further, which we will do below.

5. Learn how to analyze comparable sales reports and compute an offer.
Again, we will cover this thoroughly below.

6. Submit your first offer within 14 days.

7. Assemble the rest of your support team.

8. Put out notices on bulletin boards (internet or physical), classified ads (internet or physical) and postcards. Get creative, but, more importantly, track your sources for results.

"We buy houses for cash
Looking for properties to buy,
Will consider any and all,
Default/foreclosure OK
Call 555- 1234

This technique you read about more extensively previously. It brings results!

9. Schedule monthly stewardship interviews with yourself

You need to assess your performance, adjust your course and refine your goals on a regular basis. This will include considering adjustments to your personal vision as well as to the direction of your business. Even the most sophisticated airliner flying from New York to Los Angeles is off course 90% of the time. It's the onboard computer which allows the pilot to stay in contact with the worldwide network of beacons. The entire voyage is a series of analysis and correction of course. That is the best way our lives are, and that is the way your business will be.

With this start, if you stay with it, your future will be bright. Remember that consistency, the everyday consistent actions and tasks are the life-blood of your venture. Make sure that this includes always learning new things. Books, tapes, seminars, information from the World Wide Web should all be part of your daily business routine.

Master this, and you have mastered the business that will provide you the **greatest freedom** you can have, the freedom to be and do what you desire, without financial worry and all under your direction.

Qualifying Properties for Investment

11 Points of Information to Know

Here are 11 things you want to find out about a property over the telephone before you go visit it personally. Remember to be low key and friendly, especially if talking to the seller without an agent. It's good to start out "I'm calling about the house you have for sale. Can you tell me about it?" Then let them talk and take notes. You don't necessarily need every single point her, but, get enough information that we can decide whether to go after the property or not:

10. Size of lot (in general, for comparison).

11. Size of house (square feet).

12. Number of bedrooms/ bathrooms.

13. Special features (public transportation, fenced yard, garage, fireplace, grocery store near, etc.) or miscellaneous information (recent improvements or fix-ups).

14. Price the seller is looking for.

These first 5 are general points and can be found on the MLS, (Multiple Listing Service available from your local real estate office), but, it's still good to discuss them for the sake of building a connection to the seller. The next 6 points are designed to establish the seller's motivation:

15. Why that price? (How specific is this seller, how knowledgeable?)

16. Why is the house for sale?

17. How long has the house been on the market?

18. Does the house have a mortgage? How much? What are monthly payments? What is the interest rate?

Note: People often feel their mortgage is private information; if you are talking to a FSBO (For Sale By Owner), instead of just asking outright, ask if the mortgage is assumable. If the answer is "yes," say "great, that makes things easier. So that I know how much financing I need to get myself, could you tell me how much I can assume?" If they tell you the loan is not assumable, tell them, "that's OK, the bank will work with me, but, I need to know how much it is to give them the information." The idea is to make things more business-like and less personal. Of course, if the seller is an investor, its already business, so don't worry about the question.

19. Is the seller looking for cash at the closing?

20. Will the seller help with financing?

Point 11 helps the client find out if the seller will help finance. Problem is, many sellers don't know what seller financing is and our clients ask in such a way as to confuse or frighten the seller. Our clients should never ask a FSBO seller a question like "so tell me, would you be willing to carry a note and take back financing on this deal?" This will give the seller a vision of the client as a slick operator in a double-breasted pinstriped suit with a fat cigar driving an Eldorado Cadillac. It will make the seller nervous and nervous people don't negotiate well.

Solution: Before talking about seller financing, as "**Do you know very much about creative financing?**"
The seller usually doesn't, but, is likely embarrassed to own up to it and will say "yes." You can then continue, "**Tell me what you've heard.**" *The seller now has an opportunity to explain. Listen patiently, and then explain:*

"**In accepting creative financing, you greatly increase the number of people interested in buying your house. You make more money in selling your house and you reduce your income tax liability from the sale. I always work with a title company (lawyer, escrow company, whatever is customary in your state) that has been in the business for 15 years, so it's done legally. It's a win-in situation and works very well.**" *Note: the client should research* *to make sure the company or attorney cited really does creative financing.*

"Creative financing might include a conventional mortgage, a private lender's mortgage and a note that the seller holds secured by the home. <u>Most real estate agents don't do creative financing because they don't understand it and most banks don't work with it because they can't make any money at it.</u>"

"In essence, I give you some cash for your house, but, also make monthly payments to you for a couple of years, then give you all the rest. You collect interest on the amount I'm making payments on, so you make more money and you get income spread out over a couple of years, so you have less tax."

If you know most of this information, you can now make a decision on the value of pursuing this property – or at least whether you want to bother going across town to take a look at it.

Notes:

_____

_____

_____

_____

_____

_____

_____

_____

_____

_____

_____

_____

_____

_____

_____

_____

_____

Chapter 9: Contract Flips or Retailing

The Real Estate Investor's Role

In this role, the investor buys real estate with the intention of immediate resale for profit. The flipper gains control over properties at well below the going or "retail" rate.

In a sense, the flipper acts as both principal and middleman, buying at one price, and reselling at a higher price. In the absence of a large margin between the flipper's purchase price and the selling price, the resulting profit is close to what a real estate agent might make off the deal. But the flipper may only have a few hours of his time tied up in the deal instead of days or weeks of work. Occasional bargain purchases bring a much larger profits.

In order to do these kinds of contract flips, you need no license. You are not regulated by any government agency. (***You enjoy low overhead <u>work from home</u>***, if you wish, you only need a telephone with voice mail) and flexible working hours.

How Flipping Works

Flipping evolves through several levels, depending on experience, expertise and how much time and effort you want to put into it.

The Finder

The Finder works as a "bird dog," finding potential deals. The finder then sells the information to other investors. This can be an excellent way to get started because you don't need cash or a lot of knowledge and experience to look for distressed properties. You look at a property for sale, gather the necessary information and then provide this information to investors for a fee.

The fee varies according to the price of the property how much profit potential it shows. You can easily earn five hundred to a thousand every time another investor uses your information to purchase a property.

The Dealer

Like the Finder, the Dealer locates deals for other investors, but, takes the extra step of signing a contract for purchase of the property. When you do this, you have two options:

> ➢ ***Close on the property and turn it over for sale immediately.***
> ➢ ***Just sell the contract to another investor.***

Either way, you provide more than just information because you control the property with a binding purchase contract. If you put up earnest money to secure the deal, you assume more risk than the Finder does. On the other hand, by controlling the property with a purchase contract, your profit can be much higher.

As a Dealer, you can flip as many deals as you can find. It's not a matter of money; it's a matter of money; it's a matter of finding the deals. A successful full-time investor, can make well over fifteen thousand dollars a month without ever repairing a property or having to mess with a tenant.

On a part-time basis, a successful investor can make an extra three thousand dollars a month flipping a property or two.

The key is knowledge, dedication and a strong work ethic.

The Retailer

This is who buys the properties that Finders and Dealers locate. The Retailer fixes up the property to be sold for fair market value (i.e. retail), to whoever will be living there.

Of the three roles, the Retailer puts up the most money, bears the greatest risk and stands to make the largest profit on each deal. Part of the risk incurred stems from the time needed to rehabilitate the property and offer it for sale while dealing with carrying costs on the purchase, repair and miscellaneous expenses such as taxes and utilities. In contrast, the Finder or Dealer get paid in just a few days.

If you're just getting started in real estate and need to build your confidence and knowledge before moving on to other real estate ventures (but still need to make some extra cash), you should start with flipping contracts.

With flipping you'll be able to earn while you learn the ropes in real estate and you don't have to worry about risk if you do it right.

What is flipping? Very simply, it's contracting to purchase a property then selling your right to purchase to a third person. And, yes, it is perfectly legal in all states.

A Quick Flip Example

Here's an example of how a typical flip might work.

Let's say you find a house that is run down and vacant. It doesn't even have a for sale sign in the yard. One thing you can depend on, though: whatever you offer the owner is more than he or she is getting on this house right now.

With a little detective work (more on this later), you find the owner and negotiate a "risk free" contract to purchase the property. The price you negotiate would be better (i.e.: lower) than 60% of the value the house will have after repairs are made. You offer a very low earnest money deposit ($10.00).

The great thing is that the owner was not actively selling the house, so a minimum earnest money deposit should not create an argument and since the house was just sitting and presenting no economic value to the owner, the price you offer can be low.

As soon as you get the signed purchase contract, you contact an investor that rehabs houses in the area and offer to sell the house for $3,000 more than your contract amount. That would still put it at around 60-65% of value, which will be very attractive.

To transfer your right to buy the property at the contract amount to the investor, you fill out a one page "Assignment of Contract" form and get $500 in earnest money. A few days later the transaction closes at a title company or an attorney's office and you get a check for $3,000 PLUS your $10.00 earnest money deposit.

Does It Work?

Flipping contracts has been around for a long, long time. We've researched, studied and compiled a large volume of educational material to develop a system that works.

A Word of Caution

<u>**Persistence is vital to YOUR success**</u>. Some months you may find two, three, or more properties to flip. Other months you may not find any. You want to continually network yourself, not only to find deals to control, but, investors or even owner/occupants to take these deals off your hands. Develop new leads constantly. Some leads will work out, some won't. Some sellers will be very motivated and some won't be.

We like the attitude of *SWSWSWN*. This simple means, *"Some Will, Some Won't, So What Next."* If a homeowner chooses not to accept your terms or our offer; that is not a personal rejection of you it is a simple difference of opinion. If the seller accepts your terms, you have successfully closed a sale. But even the greatest sales people do not close every sale. Time has a way of changing everything. Learn to stick with it, even when you are discouraged.

Notes:

_____

_____

_____

_____

_____

_____

_____

_____

_____

Chapter 10: Your Support Team of Professionals

You can't do everything yourself. Some things you lack expertise for, other things you lack time for. A team will help you, because now you can delegate things that other people can do and free up your time for running your own business.

The following are people you should have on your team:

> ### Real Estate Agent

This is someone out there finding you deals. This agent will write your offers if the seller has an agent, whether your agent find the deal or you do. When you buy a property for fix-up and sale, you may give this agent the listing. The agent's incentive for working with you is the commissions received on your purchasers and sales.

In return, the agent should provide you with reports of comparable properties sold from the multiple listing service. It is good if this agent works with an agency that is registered with HUD (Dept. of Housing and Urban Development), VA (Dept. of Veterans Administration) and other government type repossessions.

> ### Mortgage Lenders

You should have contacts with several. Ask whether or not they do investor lending; ask whether they lend against the appraised value rather than the purchase price; ask whether they put together 100% packages; ask whether the have hard money; ask if they do state income, low doc (non-verified lending) or no-doc (no documentation). More details below:

- Lending against appraised value rather that purchase price indicates that they might be able to come up with $80,000 for you to buy a house worth $100,000 with no money out of pocket if you can get it for $80,000.

- 100% package means they can get all the money you need from several sources without you paying out of pocket.

- Hard money comes from private investors rather than from lending institutions; they don't have regulations to observe. It may be more expensive, but, they might only care whether this is a good deal, not how your credit or income are).

- Stated income, no-doc (no documentation) or non-verified lending means the lender looks at aspects of the deal other than your credit and income; in other words, if you have a sure money-maker, but, lousy credit and minimal income, this lender will still work with you.

- Sources – There are a lot of good sources for mortgages both locally and nationally. *Avoid having your credit report pulled an innate number of times as doing so will reduce your credit score used by banks and lending institutions to grant you a mortgage or other loan.*

➤ **A Real Estate Attorney**

This is all about asset protection; you don't want to amass your empire only to lose it to frivolous lawsuits. In certain states and in Canada, an attorney does the closing and manages the escrow. It may as well be yours.

➤ **An Accountant**

The accountant should know real estate and tax law. This is not just to get your taxes done at the end of the year; this is so you can strategize with someone who understands the impact of income taxes and capital gains on what you want to do.

➤ **An Appraiser**

Appraisers compute the market value of a property, usually for the lenders. Although you will use comparable sales reports to figure the future market value of projects for yourself, the appraiser can help you get a buy-fix-&-sell project moved quickly by getting the information you need for FHA financing for your buyers.

➤ **A Home Inspector**

You want to go after cosmetic fix-ups, not structural makeovers. The inspector will make sure it stays that way by alerting you to possible complications.

➤ **A Banker / Credit Union**

This is not just the manager of a local branch. This should be a vice president level executive with lending authority. If borrowing a quick $10,000 on your signature allows you to take advantage of a great opportunity, you will be grateful for the time it took to cultivate this relationship.

➤ **A Title Company**

If you work in a state where they are used, a title company can provide you with property reports on properties you are looking at so you know in advance if there are problems with the title. If the company knows you will be bringing business to it (closings, title insurance, etc.) people will be glad to give you the reports for free or a very nominal charge.

➤ **A Handyman (Contractor)**

The handyman will act as the general contractor for your rehab projects, someone you have tested and can trust to do good quality, honest work in a timely fashion. He can do estimates of costs for you to save you time on the front end and to ensure profitability. He can also oversee the sub-contractors.

You may be thinking of being your own handyman. If so, consider this. Would it be more cost effective for you to paint and replace floor tiles in the kitchen or would you be better off getting out and finding more deals and making more money? Or perhaps

you may consider hiring a house finder/realtor and you be the handyman either way remember plan your work and work your plan.

Example of Sub-contractors:

- ➤ A painter
- ➤ A flooring (carpet, tile & linoleum) person
- ➤ A roofer

These people can be very valuable to you in your business. Create relationships with them and keep them active. Be sure they are both licensed and insured. Obtain proof of same. It will make a great difference.

Why Does A Real Estate Investor Need A Real Estate Agent?

One of the most important assets that a new real estate investor can bring to the business is a good working relationship with a reliable real estate agent. Strangely, many new investors avoid working with agents, thinking it will be expensive. In reality, for every dollar they save in commissions, they may end up losing ten dollars in profits.

In truth, most highly successful real estate investors work very closely with real estate agents. Agents provide them a very important service. From agents they find out about the good deals out there that are posted to the **Multiple Listing Service (M.L.S.)**. The agents can also provide them reports of comparable sales, gathered from the MLS.

The M.L.S. – an important tool

Let's look at how this works. The MLS is a local database on which participating agents list the properties that they are working to sell. That allows them to share their listings with other MLS members. Now Ed at ERA Real Estate can show the perfect house for his clients, even though the house in question is listed by Suzi over at Coldwell Banker. He finds it in the MLS book or on the Internet site and has the master key or the
combination to get into the house to show it. If his clients buy, he and Suzy split the total sales commission between them.

When you work actively with several agents, they can locate properties through the MLS that specifically meets your requirements. They can particularly look for houses that fit the price range and neighborhood profile that you develop. They can look for indications of seller flexibility in the listing. Each listing agent has the option of writing something about the property, some of which show good seller motivation: "handyman special", "needs TLC", "seller will finance", "seller transferred", "price reduced" and "must sell" are excellent examples of the wording you may choose to use to advertise your real estate listings.

Using these keywords in an MLS search helps the agent focus on those types of deals you are looking for. The result can save you a lot of time, since the only properties you look at are pre-qualified. At the same time, the agent can print reports of sold properties comparable to the subject property. Since these comparables are just like the house you are looking at and they sold recently, you have a good idea of market value before you even see the property in question. Think of the time you can save by focusing only on potentially profitable deals!

How to train an agent to do it your way

Real estate agents are trained to sell houses. They are not necessarily trained to think creatively *outside the box* of traditional real estate selling has constructed. That means that you will probably have to speak with a number of agents before you get one or two who can really do the work for you. Consider the following:

1. The Pareto Principle of Economic Theory states that 80% of production comes from 20% of the effort; we alter that to say that 80% of production comes from 20% of the producers. In every field, there are those who get most of it done and the majority just follows along. This applies to real estate agents as much as to any field. In fact, of all newly licensed agents today, 80% will be out of the business in 5 years. This means that many of them will simply not be capable of helping you or not interested in doing the extra work or the work different from the way they work now. Expect that many will tell you, "you can't do that," or "that won't work." It's their loss, because working with you could represent a huge increase in their income.

2. The veteran real estate agents have bucked the odds; they were able to thrive when most couldn't and now make a comfortable living. Notice the word, "comfortable." They often have no desire to rock the boat. Things are going well, why change now? It is very likely that the only veteran willing to work with you would be one who has worked with other investors successfully in the past. On the other hand, a young rookie has not been so indoctrinated yet and still retains that enthusiasm and willingness to do new things that make him or her coach able and a good match for your business.

Since real estate agents are just humans like the rest of us, you will want to talk with a number of them while selecting those or that one that will be on your team. Remember that it is **your** team, and you call the shots. But first you will want to sell the agent on trying out for your team. We have devised a speech that helps you do this. A sales script frees you from the need to try and figure out what to say next while the other person is talking so you can pay attention. This will also help you stay in control of the conversation.

The agent shall commit to...

Once an agent has expressed willingness to try out, you should outline four different commitments you expect of the agent. Just as the coach of any sports team expects those trying out to give 100%, you may expect that of your team, as well. The upside is that if an agent spends 2-3 hours a week finding deals for you to look at, can translate into $40,000 annual income to the agent.

Here are the four commitments an agent should make to be on your team:

1. Commit to finding properties that meet your desired profile regarding:
   a. Location (low to medium income areas)
   b. Price range (somewhat below the average for that area).

2. Commit to providing you information on 3 or 4 properties every Thursday by a set time. This information will likely come from the MLS and you are entitled to a *full-page* print for each property, so that you have necessary details and information. The reason for a Thursday deadline is so you can prepare for the weekend.

3. Commit to doing key-word searches of the MLS in order to locate the properties for you to look at; this helps you pre-qualify the properties to cut down on time waste involved in looking at unsuitable properties or talking with unmotivated sellers. There are four specific types of searches you would like:
   a. Distress words: reduced (i.e., price reduced), must (i.e., must sell), transferred, moving, handyman (i.e., handyman's special), TLC (i.e., needs TLC), motivated, sacrifice, anxious.
   b. Zero down or nothing down.
   c. Seller finance (U.S.)/vendor take-back (Canada).
   d. Assumable mortgage (especially in Canada).

4. Commit to providing at least three or four valid reports of comparable sales for each of the new properties presented each week; this allows you to view the property with a pretty good idea of how much it should sell for after you pretty it up. Eventually, with experience, armed with this information, you should be able to make oral offers on the spot and save a lot of time.

If you have two or three agents fulfilling these commitments for you in various locations, you should have plenty of deals to look at. If you inspect 5 "pre-qualified" properties a week, you are in a position to make 2 or 3 offers a week (see "Making An Offer" below), which should result in at lease one excellent and profitable purchase per month. And you're on your way.

Getting a Realtor on Your Team

Be a Recruiter

It is important to present a professional and competent image when doing your own business, in order to gain credibility with clients and those who will work with you. This is no different when your business is real estate investment and you are putting together a team of people to work with you. In spite of what the people at "Sprite" would have you believe, image is far from nothing. Given that people know nothing about you at the first meeting it is all they have to go on in judging whether working with you will be worthwhile.

The following is a simple speech that may be useful in presenting yourself to a real estate agent, the first member of the team that you should assemble. Most agents will not understand what you want, because they are trained and conditioned to work differently. Your best results will probably come with relative novices (perhaps a year in the business) or with veterans who have worked with investors in the past.

"We buy properties, fix them up, then sell them again or hold on to them as rentals. We use private funding so that we can close quickly. We're looking for an agent who can check through the MLS and find properties that we can profitably invest in and then tell us about them. We will look at most of them and make offers on those that meet our needs. So we would like you to find us deals. Every time you find us a good deal, we'll put our offer through you, so you'll get your commission. If you're working with us and we find a deal ourselves, we'll still put the offer through you so you still get your commission. Whenever we want to sell something we've bought, we'll list it with you so you get another commission. If you tell us about a for-sale-by-owner deal that works for us, you'll get a bonus.

"Does this sound like something you are able to do?"

Here are a few points to keep in mind about this speech:

> ➤ Talk about yourself in the plural – it sounds more official. You alone might just be some anonymous schmuck trying to talk big, but, using the plural implies you have a whole team behind you (which you do) providing knowledge, know-how, funding and competence.

> ➤ A real estate agent's biggest fear is putting together a deal, only to see it fall apart because the buyer can't come through with the money. They will want to quiz you about your finances. At this point nothing you can say in good conscious is going to reassure them, so you don't want to tell them much. How do you avoid answering their probing questions? By applying a fundamental principle of selling: **you control the direction of the conversation by asking questions.** In other words, you don't want to be telling, you want to be asking and the agent should be telling. You are offering this agent a tryout to perhaps make your team, after all. You have a lot to offer. By working with you, this agent stands to double his or her income over the next year. Below we will have some examples of how you can handle this to your benefit.

> ➤ Another fundamental principle of selling states that people don't buy features, they buy benefits. The benefits speak to their feelings and emotions, features are just facts. You want to sell this agent on your business plan and on working with you in the way you are learning to work. That mean the agent needs to feel the benefits of working with you. That is why the final section of this speech emphasizes the benefits: "you'll get a commission, you'll still get another commission, plus you could get a bonus," etc..

> ➤ After you finish the speech, simply ask, "Does this sound like something you would be able to do?" (Don't ask if they want to, that makes it sound like there is a question about the advantage of working with you – rather, are they up to doing it, because there is no doubt what you are doing will be good for them). If they answer "yes" to your question, it is time to give them your first assignment as a member of the team. You could have them find comparable sales reports (comps) for finding the value of a property you have looked at or

they could search for good prospects on the MLS. You can delegate the activity to them by giving clear instruction of what you want a time deadline for performance:

1. We're looking at a place on Maple Avenue and we need to find out whether it's worth pursuing. We'd like you to get us some comps, printed each on the full page so we get the detail, 8 to 10 comparable properties and we'd like to have them by Thursday @ noon, if you can.
2. We want to start looking in the area between South 8th Street and South 34th Street, in the price range below $80,000. We'd like to get a list of homes in the price range. We'd like you to also get all the homes in that area that have the words "handyman," "TLC," "reduced," or "motivated" in the description. We'd like to have these lists by Thursday @ noon, if you can.

You will find that if you give these assignments to 4 different agents, you'll get four different levels of performance. Therefore, you should talk to 3 or 4 agents so that you can select the best one for you.

What if the agents keep asking questions, I don't know the answers to?

A Tutorial:

Here are some examples so how you can handle questions from a real estate agent, a mortgage broker, a lender, or any other person you need to work with. It will help you if you start by letting them know that you work with a group and that is simply your job to find the properties that the group will be investing in (If you don't have a group yet? Visit your yellow pages for groups of professionals you'd like to find properties for and do so). Go back up to the information about your support team!):

"Do you have the money for the down payment?"

"You know, the down payment money is taken care of already, but, what we want to find out, are you willing to help us find properties that we can invest in?"

"Do you have financing for this?"

"Yes, the financing is all handled, it's not a problem, but, we need to find out whether we can work with you in finding profitable deals to invest in."

"Have you been pre-qualified for financing?"

"As a matter of fact, we've got that taken care of, but, we need to find someone to work with to find profitable deals and want to know whether you can work with us."

"How's your credit?"

"Hey, this isn't about me, I'm just here to get information. But we're checking to see whether or not you want to work with us to find a lot of properties for investment purposes."

You probably see the pattern here: give a vague answer and then turn it around to a question directed toward the other person. This is how you stay in charge and avoid embarrassment.

How Can We Remove Anxiety From the Investment Property Offer Process & Ensure a Healthy Profit on the Transaction

An investor who turned 47 deals in his first year of investing tells people that he uses the MLS for nearly all his deals and makes lots of offers: out of 10 – 20 get accepted.

We as investors must make lots of offers. No offers, no deals; no deals, no money, no success. But this is hard for many people. They wonder how to make offers, how much is too much, how much is too little, will the seller take them seriously, will the agent take them seriously.

We want to take the anxiety out of making the offers so that people are willing to make 10 or 20 offers a month in order to get one project to work on. For many people, a formula for crunching the numbers helps. Then they can make an offer, even a very low offer, with a take-it-or-leave-it-attitude. I equate this with the process a building contractor goes through when bidding on a job. The methodology and systems are the same, only the outcome is different. The building wants to find the lowest amount he can charge and make a profit, the investor wants to find the highest amount he can offer and still make a profit.

With this formula, you can make your offers, knowing that if only one out of ten is accepted, the one that is accepted will produce a $5,000 to $10,000 pay per month. Now you can tell the seller or agent, "this is the figure that my computations give me. I have to make some money here or I can't afford to do the business. If I pay any more than this, I won't get my profit."

Let's look at how this all works:

Preparation for the offer

This strategy is ideally suited for the buy-fix-&-sell activities that are a good way to start out. You look for modest starter homes – the kind that first-time homebuyers are looking for. There are plenty of people with few assets and marginal credit who need a home.

This strategy also allows you to continue to grow as a real estate investor without hitting your head against the ceiling of insufficient credit and assets. When you take on a rental property for the long-term, you finance with a mortgage. Mortgages are based on the borrower's debt ratio, generally limited to around 36%, which means that eventually your debt ratio will be higher than what any lender wants to work with, unless you are able to put 65% down on all your deals.

Buy-fix-and-sell transactions are short-term deals, done without a mortgage. The property still acts as collateral, but, the loan is short-term – less than a year and is normally not reported to credit bureaus. Meanwhile, each project puts $5,000 - $10,000 in capital back into the business. Sufficient capital will allow mortgage application to be considered on the basis of business cash flow, not personal debt ratio.

There are three foundation legs of the offer:

> ➤ Information about the seller's motivation, derived from the 11 points of information (see above).
> ➤ The cost of rehab, based on inspection and analysis of material costs and time.
> ➤ The amount the house can be sold for after rehab, which we call the Future Market Value (FMV).

Computing Market Value

The future market value is the foundation of the offer. It starts with an accurate appraisal of value. We say future market value because we want to know how much we can expect to sell the house for after we complete the work on it. Our interest is in how much this house will be worth when it is shiny new looking.

Obviously, this involves looking into the future with a bit of conjecture. Our only recourse is to see what other homes that are *just like this one* have actually sold for in the recent past. To know this, you need to get reports of comparable sales, also called *comps.* Your real estate agent can provide these easily from the MLS. You should obtain at least 8-10 comps that are very similar to the house you are considering. Instruct the realtor to print out a full-page report for each individual property, rather than combining 8 or 10 to a page. This way you get the detail you need and a description that the listing wrote about the house that sold.

1. Rank the Comparables

Once you have 8-10 comps, rank them from 1-10, using the following criteria. These criteria are shown here according to priority, with #1 receiving far greater weight than the others:

> ➤ Same bedroom/bathroom count
> ➤ Same neighborhood
> ➤ Same building style (two story, bungalow, tri-level, etc.)
> ➤ Close in age

Your highest ranked comparable most closely resembles the subject property. Now discard all but top 5 (and discard #5 if it's not good enough) and look at only those that you feel are just like the subject house, the one you want to buy.

2. Compute the Cost-Per-Square-Foot

The next step involves getting a cost-per-square-foot for each comparable. First divide the total living square footage of comp #1 into its sales price, (EXAMPLE: 1,142 sq. ft. into $87,000 = $76 rounded off). This equalizes all comps for comparison. After you have done this for all the comparables you are using, then find the average cost-per-square-foot for all. Add the five cost-per-square-foot figures together and divide the total by 5. This is your average cost-per-square-foot. Now take this figure and multiply it by the square footage of the subject house. This is the future market value of the subject house and provides the foundation of the offer formula.

The Offer Formula

Start with the FMV

> Subtract profit amount
> Should be at least 10% of FMV or $10,000, whichever is less.
> This is the reason for doing the deal.
> Subtract rehab costs.
> Subtract acquisition and carrying costs.
> > Closing costs.
> > Six months of property taxes.
> > Six months of property insurance.
> > Six months of utilities.
> > > Six month figures ensure no shortage.
> Subtract cost of money.
> > We don't yet know how much must be borrowed.
> > > Take 75% of FMV.
> > > Multiply this figure by 18% and divide by 2.

Here's a Sample Formula Computation:

	FMV	**= $85,000**
Profit		(8,500)
Rehab		(8,000)
Carrying		(1,100)
Interest		(5,738)
Offer		**$61,662**

Conclusion:

If the seller is asking $85,000 and you offer $61,000, the seller might just reject your offer. However, would you want to pay $85,000 for this house, or even $75,000? It needs work and that work will cost $8,000 by itself. Even if we sell it in a month, you will pay nearly $1,000 for the interest. Even if you can negotiate away your closing costs, buying this property for $75,000 will not return you a profit. On the other hand, if you make enough offers, you will meet up with enough highly motivated sellers to make this work. The result of this offer, if accepted, would be a minimum profit of $8,500, more if you can sell the house in less than six months. Now you can have the confidence to make lots of offers.

Finding a Mortgage Expert For Your Team

Finding a house to buy is one thing. Financing it is another. That is not to say that it can't be done. We just don't expect that you have it sitting in a money market account somewhere. And since most of us don't have all the money we need to do all the deals we might want to do, we must orient ourselves toward the concept of **OPM** to fund our projects.

OPM is simply other people's money. Without it, we would sooner or later run out of gas and our investing could go no further.

The good news is that no matter where you go in the world, there are people who have money – a lot of money – more money than they need. They also most likely subscribe to the philosophy that it is easier for them to put their money to work for them than it is to work for their money. In other words, if you have the deal that will make more money for these money sources, they will want to give you money.

It has been said that you can have anything you want if you will help enough other people get what they want. What these people with money want is ways to get more money without having to do much work. If you do the work and they put up the money, both of you win, because you both get money.

Is it really possible to tap into this money-source? Check the classified section of your Sunday newspaper and look for ads about money to lend. Notice how many of them carry the message that if you can fog a mirror, we'll lend you money. It's there; you just need to find it.

How to find it? As with any other commodity that is in high demand but short supply, there are brokers whose business consists of creating a network of money sources of all kinds, so that if someone needs funding, they can supply that need. These mortgage brokers always have an ad in the yellow pages, so this would be a logical place to start. Simply call the mortgage companies that you find under the listing "Mortgage" in the yellow pages. Make sure you are talking to a loan officer. Tell the officer, "we buy properties to fix them up then sell them again or hold on to them as rentals. We're looking for funding for our deals and wanted to see if we could work with you. Do you mind if I ask a couple of questions?"

Remember to have fun with this. Be cheerful. Watch yourself in a mirror as you talk to make sure you are smiling. Be friendly, because people prefer to do business with people they like. Remember too, that just as with any other group of people, 95% of all mortgage brokers are more or less coasting, going through the motions to do the minimum needed to get by. Only 5% are prepared to go the extra mile, having both the knowledge and the ambition to give you what you need. Don't be discouraged if many of them can't help you. You might hear a lot of "no, we can't / don't do that." All you need is a couple of brokers who are willing to do whatever it takes to get things taken car of and you are on your way.

Remember, too, that mortgage brokers are paid on commission. If they don't place a loan for you, they don't get paid. You need not be nervous about talking to them or taking up their time. They live to talk to potential clients. If they don't keep finding new clients, their business will die. Believe that they want to talk to you!

Here are some questions to ask: (Refer to glossary below)
  - ➢ **What percentage of a deal will you finance?**
  - ➢ **Can you lend against the appraised value rather than the purchase price?**
  - ➢ **Do you do piggyback loans?**
  - ➢ **Will you allow the seller to take back a 2ⁿᵈ for the down payment?**
  - ➢ **Do you have hard money to lend against rehabs?**
  - ➢ **Do you do stated-income or no-doc lending? (Meaning they don't need to document your income or credit, they take your work for it – you state it, it is so).**

You probably won't get all yeses from any one broker, but, you will get a feel for how liberal and willing the person is by how they answer. It may take playing the Columbo role for a while, asking a bunch of questions to draw the information out from the person.

All you are doing right now is getting together a list of people who sound like they might be willing to work with you. At this point you have nothing to present to them, anyway. Nobody is going to give you money on the terms you need it until you have a deal to show him or her. Hard money is lent based on the value of the collateral, not based on your income or creditworthiness. They want to know what the deal is before they commit. For now, just find out that you will talk to when you have a deal. When you have a deal to present, you can present your packet to 3 or 4 and see that comes up with the best offer.

Then you are on your way to a big payday.

Lending Glossary:

➤ *Loan to value ratio (LTV):* the percentage of the properties fair market value that is lent, i.e.: FMV= $100,000, divided by the loan amount =$65,000, LTV=65%.

➤ *Appraised value:* Fair market value as set by an appraisal – a loan of 80% of an appraised value of $100,000 would be $80,000; if you can get the seller to agree to an $80,000 purchase price, you have 100% of what you will need to make this purchase.

➤ *Piggyback loan:* A first mortgage is funded up to a certain percentage of the purchase price (you pay $80,000 for the first $100,000 home with a first mortgage of $64,000 – representing 80% LTV). A second mortgage is funded for 20% LTV of the purchase price (i.e.: $16,000). The total is $80,000, enough to **do the deal with no cash out of pocket**. This also happens to be 80% of appraised value.

➤ *Quit claim deed:* A document that transfers title of ownership from one person to another. If I wanted to gift you my house, I would use a quitclaim deed. *Must be handled with your local real estate attorney.*

➤ If the seller takes back a 2nd mortgage, you can get 80% from the bank ($64,000 on a $100,000 house), then sign a second mortgage with the seller for $16,000. You will then make monthly payments to the seller and another monthly payment to the bank. The seller gets $80,000 on the sale, but, $16,000 is paid over a period of years.

➤ *Hard money:* Money from non-institutional lenders, usually groups of investors or individual investors with lots of money. These loans are usually short-term – one year or less and are based on the value of the collateral, not on your creditworthiness. These are ideal for short term buy-fix and –sell deals.

➤ *Stated income or no-doc lending:* The lender doesn't need to document your income or credit, but, take your word for it – you state it, it is so.

Chapter 11: PRE-FORECLOSURES

Great deals just waiting to happen

When people talk about purchasing foreclosures they may be talking about:

> **Pre-foreclosure**: When you are dealing with the owner of the property that is in foreclosure.

> **Purchasing a property at an auction.** Attending an auction, sheriff sale, trust deed sale, where the lender is foreclosing on the property and forcing a sale of the property.

> **After auction when the property has been foreclosed on and is owned by the bank.**
>   - Foreclosure
>   - REO – Real Estate Owned (by the bank)
>   - Special Asset (sometimes called that by the bank)

The Steps (System) for Buying Pre-foreclosures

1- Find the foreclosure.
2- Contact the owner.
3- Determine Value.
4- Analyze and Inspect Property.
5- Negotiate.
6- Sign Contract.
7- Check Title.
8- Fix Up and Rent or Sell.

Sources To Find Foreclosures:

> **Court house.**
> **Title Company.**
> **Legal Publication or newspaper.**
> **Subscription Lists.**
> **Internet.**
> **Sign Contract.**
> **Check Title.**
> **Fix Up and Rent or Sell.**

The Courthouse:

The sale of the property, auction or foreclosure takes place at the courthouse. The foreclosure process is systematic and a well-defined process. At regular times of the day and week, the court auctions off the property (the sale). You can find out the times by simply calling the office and asking the clerk. You may have heard the statement that the property "was sold on the courthouse steps." Most often it actually happens in the lobby, foyer or a specified location indoors out of the weather.

A Typical sale would involve:

- ➢ A scheduled time for properties to be sold.
- ➢ A clerk making an announcement of file case numbers and their status (solved, available, etc.)
- ➢ A clerk listing the case and/or property description and asking for bids.
- ➢ The bidding starts and a winner will obtain the property based on highest bidder.
- ➢ The property is bought and paid for at the courthouse.

The property will usually have at least one bidder. The lender wants to ensure the property is sold for at least what is owed on the property. Therefore the lender or their designate starts the bidding at the amount being foreclosed on. If that is the only bid, the auction is over. The lender will actually receive the money so there is no real cost. There have been the occasional errors where the lender did not protect their debt and a bidder other than the lender received the property for a song. If there are multiple bidders the process can be quite entertaining.

We suggest very strongly that you go and visit the courthouse and watch several auctions before you participate. You will learn a lot about the process. You may even try to get to know some of the individuals at the foreclosure. Banks, lawyers, agents, investors, title company representatives and more will oftentimes be in attendance. They are all excellent contracts for the investor. If you own a property, check the documents while you are at the courthouse. Just ask the clerks. It will help if you have the legal description. Get it from your mortgage documents. Also review the bulletin boards in the offices and pick up any publications and notices in the offices. Check the Lis Pendens list (legal notice of foreclosures).

In deed-of-trust states, the process is a little different. The trustees controlling title of the property can control the location of the sale, which may or may not be at the courthouse. Usually the trustees publish notices of sale location.

How Can You Profit from a Foreclosure?

There are a lot of opportunities for profit in foreclosures. Certainly you can buy a property during the foreclosure process prior to sale at a discount. As the foreclosure clock is counting down to the sale time, there are great deals and negotiations. Here are a couple of examples:

1- Joint venture with the owner. The owner may have had a temporary setback. They could have a substantial amount of equity in the property. Perhaps you can approach them to solve the current problem. Get their payments back on track and save their personal credit profile. In return you might agree to take 30-50% ownership of the property. Alternatively, you could agree to sell the property and get cash out for both you and the owner. In this case you would want to get to the owner early in the foreclosure process.

2- Look for properties with substantial equity. Usually the lender is going to make a bid just over the loan value to ensure the debt is paid. However, the property may have a lot of equity. Therefore you can pick the property up for a major discount and resell the home.

3- Approach the successful auction winner and inquire if they would like to sell the property, perhaps on a lease option or an installment sale.

Anita John

How to find foreclosure deals?

There are numerous ways to find foreclosures properties. Listed below are some of the most common:

> - Classified Sections
> - Legal newspapers
> - Attorneys
> - For Sale By Owners
> - Realtors
> - Auction Companies
> - Banks – ROE departments
> - U.S. Marshall's Service
> - Listing Services
> - IRS auctions
> - Bankruptcies
> - Probate Court
> - Your own advertising
> - County Courthouse, town hall or registry of deeds
>   - Check for "new cases"
>   - Check for "sale" files *

* Courthouse Research

Information you are looking for can usually be found in the Clerk of the Court's office or Land Records Department start by calling the County Courthouse to find where real estate property records are located. Each courthouse has different methods of filing documents, some in large books, some on microfiche files and others on computers.

It is important to ask a county employee for assistance. They can show you where real estate property records are located. They can show you where to start your search and where you can get more detailed information when you locate a potential suitable property. You may want to start with the lis pendens files or the docket sheet, where the most recent court actions are first recorded.

Write down the foreclosure case number and then review the file to gather data about the foreclosure. All the information concerning the title to a property is public record. Remember, only recorded information in the public records can enforce the priority and is established by the date and time of recording.

To check on deed information, visit the Tax Assessor's office or in another part of the Courthouse. Locate the correct volume and page to find the deed. The deed will show the owner's name, give a legal description of property and will have a map or plat book and page that shows the physical plat of the property.

In many instances, you will find a mortgage on the pages following the deed. From the mortgage document you can determine the type of financing, original loan amount, interest rate, legal description, date of first payment, procedure for foreclosure, assumable or non-assumable indicators and any prior liens.

If other liens are found, recheck them in the appropriate Deed Book. These are going to have to be dealt with if the property is to be purchased before the foreclosure sale.

➢ Buying the junior position lien is a way to get your foot in the door.
➢ When in 2ⁿᵈ position you have the right to protect your interest by bringing the 1ˢᵗ mortgage current in order to stop the foreclosure.

Foreclosure on the 2ⁿᵈ: Check to see if this is applicable to the state you live in. Some states have a period of redemption and other laws that may prevent you from doing this.

Finding Great Deals Through Foreclosure

When you hear the word "foreclosure" what comes to your mind? Do you cringe and slump over as if someone hit you in the stomach? Do you think of all the stories you have heard about neighbors being displaced?

We are going to change that attitude, NOW! We are excited about the tremendous opportunities in this field of real estate investing and we will also make you aware of how you can help people out AND make lots of money in the process.

First, let's talk about how foreclosures happen and we will explain how you can prosper.

It has been documented that, on a national basis, the number of foreclosures has increased every year for the past seven years. Why is this true? Corporate layoffs, downsizing and outsourcing have run rampant in the economy. These conditions cause people to get behind in their payments and the foreclosure clock starts ticking. Even though the foreclosure process allows the owner some time to cure the situation, many times the people do not have the financial resources to do so.

Why do they lack the resources? It may be because of:

➢ A loss of job.
➢ Financial crisis – the need for immediate cash.
➢ Business failure.
➢ Divorce.
➢ Death of one of the property owners.
➢ Medical problems.
➢ The increase of payments due to an adjustable rate mortgage.
➢ Balloon payments on seller-held mortgages.
➢ Job transfer and the problems associated with two mortgage payments.
➢ A temporary negative cash flow situation.
➢ Out of town or out of state owners.

These circumstances create a high profit potential for investors in what is called "The Hidden Market." It is so called because people do not understand it. The uninformed public does not know where to find the information that makes these situations viable opportunities. In addition to the hidden aspects, you have highly motivated owners who do not want to lose their homes and lenders who do not want to own the property.

In order to take advantage of the situation, we have created a system that is truly a WIN-WIN situation. The owner gets to stay in his home, the lender is brought current and you make MONEY! Let us take you through the process.

Discovering Foreclosure Opportunities

How do you find out about the foreclosures? The first thing that you must determine is whether you are in a Mortgage or a Deed of Trust State. The foreclosure process and the method of giving public notice are distinctly different.

Mortgages: In a mortgage State, the mortgage is used as the security instrument. The property owner, (the mortgagor) borrows money from the lender (the mortgagee). The mortgagor pledges the property as collateral for the loan. The owner holds the deed. If the owner becomes delinquent in making the monthly payments, the lender must file a lawsuit in the Public Records in order to start the foreclosure action. This is called a judicial action and can take a great deal of time depending on the laws of the State in which the property is located.

During this time, the Owner has every opportunity to bring the loan current. If the Owner fails to make up the back payments, the Court can rule in favor of the Lender and set a time that the property will be auctioned, usually referred to as a Sheriff's sale.

Since the lawsuits are filed in the Public Records, the information is available to every one. Locate the Clerk of the Circuit Court and ask where foreclosure complaints are filed. Once the foreclosure is filed, you can follow it by writing down the case number and reviewing the file. All of the documents will be included in these files. Once you have done this a few times, it will become easy for you. Additional information on the property can be found in the Land Records Office. It may be referred to by another name, such as the County Recorder's Office or the County Clerk's Office. You are looking for where deeds, mortgages and similar documents are recorded. You can then determine if there are any liens, judgements or other encumbrances recorded against the property.

Deed of Trust: In a Deed of Trust State, the Deed of Trust is the security instrument. There are three parties involved – the Owner (Trustor), the Lender (Beneficiary) and the Trustee (usually an attorney or a title company with an attorney). Title to the property remains in the Trustee's possession. If the Owner falls behind in the making of the payments, the Lender notifies the Trustee to record a Notice to Default at the courthouse (although this varies by state and in some states there is no requirement to file the Notice of Default). This is a non-judical method, so no lawsuit needs to be filed. After the mandated period of public notice, the property may be auctioned.

In either Mortgage or Deed of Trust states, public notice is normally required. You may read about the foreclosures in advertisements, either in the local paper or in a legal paper published by the County or City, or find it posted in the court house. *Another valuable source of this information is commercial service companies, who send out periodic lists of foreclosures for a fee.* Many of these services contain detailed information about the foreclosures, which can save valuable time and effort on your part.

The Foreclosure Process

Each state has a specific system – a step-by-step process for the lender and the owner to follow in the foreclosure process. It is a good idea to understand the specifics of your state's process and the nuances.

How The Property Is Held

Generally, real estate is secured by either a debt or a lien often called title theory or lien theory. Title

Theory states classifies the mortgage or trust deeds for properties are contract law applies. The contract conveys the title to the property secured by the underlying debt. In lien theory states, the mortgage or trust deed is a lien against the property. A lien just means an entity (usually a bank) has a claim or hold on a property as security for debt. Liens are an encumbrance to the property and recorded against the property. You may have more than just one lien (debt) against a particular property.

How Property is Foreclosed On

The lender follows a specific system of foreclosure to repossess the property or rectify the satisfaction of the debt. The States are split approximately 50/50 on the process.

First, there is Power of Sale. A good portion of the trust deed States uses Power of Sale. Power of Sale ends to be a less expensive and quicker way to foreclose on a property. Under Power of Sale the Lender (trustee) informs the property owner the debt has not been paid and specifies due date. In a few weeks if payment is not processed a stronger demand for the payment is issued, often an immediate demand for payment. States regulate the period of time prior to public auction, approximately four weeks.

The process is sometimes complicated by FHA and VA properties. The federal government, through its respective programs, guarantees these properties. The programs have their own regulations and procedures for rectifying the debt obligation and listing of the properties. You will want to gain a deeper understanding of the FHA and VA process. There are some outstanding opportunities in the FHA and VA foreclosure market. Contact your local branch office for more information.

Judicial Foreclosure governed by the courts accounts for the other half of our nation's foreclosures. Note the Power of Sale States usually have some form of judicial procedure.

Although slightly different in approach both systems have essentially seven steps:

> **Non-Payment:** From time to time we all may be a little late in our mortgage payments. The penalty for being late may be a $10 or $20 late fee and perhaps a mention on our credit report beyond two weeks the lender starts to get a little anxious. They may let a month slide, with notice of non-payment, but, very quickly they begin to take the non-payment very seriously. The second month they will send notification of past due and approximately six to eight weeks after the non-payment you can expect the phone to start to ring. The lender will try to solve the problem and work out a plan for repayment.

> **Default:** If payments continue to go unpaid, the note is moved to a default setting and legal action is initiated. There is a demand letter asking for full and immediate restitution of the debt owed or the attorneys will file suit to foreclose.

> **Lis Pendens:** After default a Lis Pendens (legat notice, literally "pending suit") is filed against the property. The Lis Pendens will include the following: case number (assigned by the court), Lender (plaintiff), owner(s) (defendants), property, legal description, notice of foreclosure and the attorney for the plaintiff.

- ➢ **Complaint:** This lists the events that took place to force foreclosure. A detailed listing of the mortgage amounts owed, time frame of non-payment, listing of the parties and property, a complete history of the mortgage and reference to the official documents. At this point the note is accelerated. The entire amount of the mortgage and related costs become fully due and payable immediately.

- ➢ **Judgment:** Final judgment occurs after a set period of time determined by the laws of the State. The defendant can still rectify the situation by paying the default. All fees have to be paid, including non-payment court fees and legal costs. That does not mean negotiations can't happen (by the owner or an investor). The lender will file a motion for judgment. When final judgment is granted the plaintiff has the right to sell the property.

- ➢ **Sale:** After the judgment the motion of sale is put into action. An order for the sale is processed and a specific date for public auction is set.

- ➢ **Redemption Period:** The process of foreclosure can take anywhere from three months to a year from start to sale. Note that during this time the legal fees and costs are escalating and being attached to the property. However, an investor can acquire the property at any point during this period. Obviously earlier would be more favorable than later (due to fewer legal expenses and mounting costs). It changes by state, but, generally investors can intervene up until the day of the sale. At the auction, a bidding war can erupt. It's good to get possession before that.

Contacting The Owners
- ➢ *In Person*
- ➢ *Send Letters and postcards*
- ➢ *Make Phone Calls*

How to Contact The Owner In Person

- ➢ Gentle approach
    - ○ Knock on door and introduce yourself
    - ○ Tell them that you really like the area and are looking to buy a house
    - ○ Tell them that someone told you that their home might be available for sale

- ➢ Direct approach
    - ○ Let them know that you noticed that their house is in pre-foreclosure
    - ○ Let them know that you may be able to help them
    - ○ Ask them if they have considered selling their home

Determining Value

- ➢ Pre-foreclosure is the best time to buy if there is equity
    - ○ Rule of thumb – Never pay more than 80% of value
    - ○ *Minimum of 20% equity after fix up*; 40% before fix up.

- ➢ Figure equity by taking the FMV (determined by comps) and subtracting:
    - ○ Principle balance

- o All costs to bring the loan current and stop foreclosure which may include the following:
  - ➤ Back payments
  - ➤ Attorney fees
  - ➤ Court costs
  - ➤ Penalty fees
  - ➤ ***Real estate taxes unpaid***   *Takes primary lien position if*
  - ➤ ***Water and sewer charges unpaid***   *Takes primary lien position if*
  - ➤ Any other lien and/or judgments   (40% before fix up)
  - ➤ Fix up costs   (20% after fix up)

Talking and Negotiating With The Owner

- ➤ Try and find out what their needs are
  - o Do they want to stay?
  - o Do they want to go?

- ➤ Sometimes the owner is in denial-help, the owner faces the fact that he/she will lose the property
  - o Loose the roof over his/her head
  - o Loose all the equity that has built up
  - o Loose any chance of having decent credit for ever (10-12) years.

- ➤ If they are willing to talk, try and find out what is happening and then try and find a solution
  - o Get them to tell you why they stopped making payments
  - o Do they have a place to go?
  - o Are people hounding them for money?
  - o Do they need money to bring utilities current?

- ➤ Sometimes they are just going to walk and will quit claim it to you to save their credit

- ➤ Let them know what you can do for them
  - o Can reinstate (bring current) the loan
  - o Stop foreclosure and save their credit
  - o Can pay their 1st months rent and deposit
  - o Can pay their utility bills so they can have utilities at new place
  - o Could give them money once they moved out

- ➤ The main thing they need to understand is that you need to stop the foreclosure
  - o Have them sign the deed (quit claim or warranty deed)
  - o Bring it current and stop the foreclosure
  - o Make the monthly payments until you can get a new loan/ lease purchaser

Making the Offer

- ➢ Using the information gathered make an offer

    - o Control your risks, Contract should include escape clauses, for instance, *sale is:*
        - ▪ Contingent upon buyer's partner's approval
        - ▪ Contingent upon buyer's approval of title report
        - ▪ Contingent upon buyer's approval of inspection of property

    - o Create a contract that spells out the terms that you have negotiated with the owner – sometimes you create that contract during the negotiation.

    - o Sign the contract and quickly go to the court house and do a title search
        - ▪ If the title looks good – order a title report
        - ▪ If you have found a lot of liens and judgments, get out of the contract

- ➢ Be sure to and get a letter authorizing you to talk and negotiate with the lender and/or attorney concerning the mortgage. Have the seller sign the document.

How To Find Owner If Property Is Vacant

- ➢ Talk to neighbors
- ➢ Check county assessor's office to see if it has a different mailing address than the house that is being foreclosed on
- ➢ If address is the same
    - o Mail two letter – 1st one addresses to the owner at the vacant address
    - o Mail 2nd letter addressed the same way, but writ in bold letter across the top of the letter:
        - ▪ **ADDRESS CORRECTION REQUESTED, DO NOT FORWARD**
- ➢ Call everyone in the phone book with the same last name

No Equity?

- ➢ If there is no equity, more than likely it is because there are liens in junior position?
    - o Approach 2nd and 3rd positions, etc. and see if they would discount the note
    - o Sometimes will sell for pennies on the $
    - o Can create equity by the discounting of the note

Notes:

_____

_____

_____

_____

_____

_____

_____

_____

_____

_____

_____

Chapter 12 – Presenting Your Investment Opportunity For Joint-Venture Consideration

Properly presenting your good deal for joint-venture consideration is essential to having your Advisory Team approve your deal in a timely fashion. Your "Investment Package" must be assembled as outlined for easy review by your Advisory Team. This not only demonstrates your ability to be professional, but, confirms your capacity for accurately compiling the details associated with real estate.

This chapter outlines the necessary requirements and guidelines for presenting your good deal for joint-venture consideration. You must follow the precise format described. It is vitally important to complete and submit all pertinent deal-qualifying forms to enable your Advisory Team to make a final joint-venture decision. Your Advisory Team is always available to assist and direct your efforts… not complete your paperwork. Therefore take the required time to professionally prepare your investment package. This practice will soon become habit, which will significantly enhance your skills and ability to become a financially successful distressed property locator.

Send your completed "Investment Package" directly to your Advisory Team via the following delivery methods: US Certified Mail, U.S. Priority Mail, United Parcel Service, or Federal Express. Avoid sending your package through regular first class mail. This helps avoid the possibility of delays or loss.

NOTE: DO NOT FAX any information to our Headquarters unless specifically requested by your Advisory Team. All non-requested facsimiles will be promptly discarded.   No deals are considered received if sent via FAX!

Let us help you create wealth

REQUIRED DOCUMENTATION:

ITEM #1: Investment Package Cover Sheet and Checklist

When presenting your good deal to your Advisory Team, you must complete the "Investment Package Checklist," and include it as the first page of your proposal. As you finish each of the following items required in your "Investment Package," check off each item as being completed and enclosed. The "Checklist" ensures that no pertinent information is forgotten, and that your good deal will be promptly submitted to your Advisory Team for review and approval for joint-venture.

ITEM #2: Market Study Worksheet

The 'Market Study Worksheet" must be completed in its entirety. No spaces are to remain blank! The information provides your Advisory Team with the critical factors that affect market conditions as well as the AVERAGE selling price of comparable properties listed and/or sold in the same neighborhood. The information is NOT intended to represent a professional appraisal of the property – only a general overview of realistic market conditions. This accounts for why you must only use comparable sales and listings that fall with a + or – 20% price range of each other when completing your "Market Study Worksheet." Properties above or below these ranges are not considered valid and will not be accepted.

Your personal comments are required in the appropriate places, therefore, please take the time to thoroughly complete the form with all pertinent information that may effect a final purchase decision.

ITEM #3: Purchase Offer Analysis Form

The "Purchase Offer Analysis Form" is designed to quickly calculate the amount of money you should offer a seller. Make certain to double-check your calculations for accuracy before submitting a written Purchase Offer.
Most importantly, make certain the "Equity-to-Cash Ratio" satisfies the minimum 40%. Remember to us $5,000 as your estimated closing costs (for 1-2 family units, and $10,000 for 3-4 family units). Also, remember that your offer is based on Future Value After Repairs; not asking price or the value of the property in it's current condition.
In the event you pursue expensive property where closing costs can be much higher than average, your Advisory Team may request that you submit additional information in order to calculate more accurate closing costs associated with purchasing and re-selling the subject property.

ITEM #4: Property Information Form

The "Property Information Form" provides your Advisory Team with pertinent facts regarding the proposed property. The required information is useful because it provides a comprehensive flavor of the location, condition, taxes, utilities, etc. of the property. Make certain you do not omit information because you will ultimately have to supply it before the project can be approved for joint venture.

The information required to complete this form can usually be obtained from <u>the real estate agent/or owner</u>. If either agent or owners are unavailable to supply all the information, check with your local court house or tax office. These are great sources of information.

ITEM #5: A Written Repair Cost Estimate from a Reputable Contracting Company

It is required to submit a comprehensive written repair cost estimate from a reputable, responsible contractor whom you have selected to complete the renovation. The estimate must be itemized room-by-room in a clear, professional, understandable format. The contractor <u>must substantiate</u> that he has <u>valid Workman's Compensation and Liability Insurance</u> in order to become the approved contractor. A sample of a cost estimate contract follows this section. Use it as a guideline for your contractor to follow. Make certain the estimates in your "Property Inspection Report" are consistent with the contractor you have selected to do the work. This helps in your ability to closely determine repair costs and eliminate any confusion or inconsistencies with repairs and costs.

NOTE: Property rehabilitation is not an exact science. In some cases, there is the possibility of hidden defects or damages which can add an extra 20%, and possibly more, to repair costs of a project. Taking the precaution of having at least two (2) qualified contractors inspect the property will reduce the possibility of incurring unanticipated costs due to hidden damages. Ask lots of questions!

ITEM #6: Contractor Information Form

The "Contractor Information Form" will supply information needed for your Advisory Team to immediately open a line of communication with the contractor who will be doing the repairs. This enables your Advisory Team to work closely with the contractor to confirm critical information and verify the progress of repairs. Please provide a copy of contractors' license, liability and workman's compensation insurance policies. Ensure all expiration dates are valid.

ITEM #7: Copy of the Purchase Offer Form

The "Purchase Offer Form" must be completed and signed by both the purchaser and the seller before the property can be considered for joint-venture consideration. Your Advisory Team cannot finalize your "Investment Package" until the seller has signed the Purchase Offer Form.

If your Realtor requires you to present your Purchase Offer on a Realtor Agreement, make certain to incorporate the appropriate 'Inspection of the Property' clause (see sample). For submission purposes, a signed Realtor contract may serve as a proper substitute for a "Purchase Offer Form."
All agreements should be made in your name and the seller's name only (meaning, all parties who have equitable interest in the property). However, before signing a Realtor contract, be sure to call your Advisory Team for further instructions.

The purchase price on the "Purchase Offer Form" should be no greater than the amount indicated on the "Purchase Offer Analysis Form," and the minimum equity-to-cash ratio should be 40%.

A verbal agreement of a purchase price is not acceptable. Only a written agreement is considered valid. Remember, do not proceed to complete extensive due diligence on a property until you have received a signed agreement from the seller. Do not waste your time on verbal agreements.. get it in writing!

ITEM #8: Photographs of Inside and Outside of Building

Submit not less than *nine* 3" x 5" full color photographs with your investment package of the subject property. Send only original photos – do not send photocopies. Photograph the front and back, and all areas requiring major repairs. Use common sense when determining how many and what type of photos to send. Remember, the photos provide your Advisory Team with visual appreciation of the property and substantiate that you have physically visited the property and conducted a complete inspection.

ITEM #9: Photographs of Comparable Sales

You must also provide exterior photographs (front view only) of all comparable sales listed on your "Market Study Worksheet." This will lend even greater credibility to your diligence in putting together your "Investment Package," and will support that your comparable sales were not strictly computer generated. The photographs confirm that you have taken the time and effort to physically visit each property to verify you have listed a legitimate comparable sale.

Important note:

Upon submission of Item #'s 9 and 10, photocopy the sample formats provided at the end of this section, and insert your photographs as indicated.

Anita John

Notes:

_____

_____

_____

_____

_____

_____

_____

_____

_____

_____

_____

_____

Appendix/ Forms Contents

!!! Thank you For your Support!!!

** **Email for FREE download,** bwic777@yahoo.com

RE Investment Package Cover Sheet and Checklist

Acquisitions Advisor Name: _____

Associate Name: _____

Address:_____

City: _____ State: _____ Zip: _____

Day Phone: _____ Evening Phone: _____

Subject Property Address: _____

City: _____ State: _____ Zip: _____

Real Estate Broker Name: _____

Real Estate Agent Name: _____

Day Phone: _____ Evening Phone: _____

Check off the following items upon completion:

- o   ITEM #1   R.E. Investment Package Cover Sheet and Checklist
- o   ITEM #2   Market Study Worksheet
- o   ITEM #3   Purchase Offer Analysis Form
- o   ITEM #4   Property Information Form
- o   ITEM #5   Property Inspection Report
- o   ITEM #6   Written Repair Cost Estimate from _____ Construction Company
- o   ITEM #7   Contractor Information Form
- o   ITEM #8   Copy of the Purchase Offer Form
- o   ITEM #9   Photographs of Inside and Outside of Subject Property
- o   ITEM #10   Photographs of Comparable Sales (Exterior)

DO NOT WRITE BELOW THIS LINE

OFFICIAL USE ONLY:

Date received: _____ Approved: yes_____ no_____

Authorized Signature: _____

Return to Associate: Date: _____ Reason: _____

Direct "Investment Package" to: Code: _____

TH _____ KB _____ FJ _____ AC _____ AJ _____

PROPERTY INSPECTION

By: _____ Date: _____

( ) SINGLE FAM. RES.   #_____ BEDROOMS #_____ BATHROOMS

PROPERTY ADDRESS: _____

GENERAL PROPERTY INFORMATION:

( ) SINGLE FAM. RES.   #_____ BEDROOMS   #_____ BATHROOMS
( ) DUPLEX 2-FAM RES.   #_____ BEDROOMS   #_____ BATHROOMS
( ) TRI-PLEX 3-FAM RES.   #_____ BEDROOMS   #_____ BATHROOMS
( ) QUAD-PLEX 4 FAM. RES. #_____ BEDROOMS   #_____ BATHROOMS
( ) MULTI- FAMILY   #_____ BEDROOMS   #_____ BATHROOMS

( ) SINGLE LEVEL   ( ) PAVED ROAD   ( ) OCCUPIED
( ) TWO STORY   ( ) DIRT ROAD   ( ) VACANT
SCHOOLS:_____

FEATURES OF HOME:
( ) FIREPLACE(S) #_____   ( ) GARAGE-SINGLE-DOUBLE
( ) LAKE FRONT   ( ) CAR PORT-SINGLE-DOUBLE
( ) SWIMMING POOL   ( ) CORNER LOT
( ) JACUZZI   ( ) COVERED PATIO
( ) CEILING FANS   ( ) SCREENED PORCH
( ) INTERCOM SYSTEM   ( ) GARAGE DOOR OPENER
( ) IRRIGATION SYSTEM

( ) SPECIAL FEATURES: _____

_____

_____

AGE OF HOME _____   APPROX. SQ. FOOTAGE _____
LOT SIZE _____   ANNUAL TAXES   _____

COMMENTS ONCONDITION:
ROOF _____   YARD/LANDSCAPE_____
APPEARANCE/PAINT_____ OTHER_____
LIST VISIBLE/TERMITE DAMAGE_____
IMPROVEMENTS TO BE COMPLETED:_____
NUMBER OF NEIGHBORHOOD LISTINGS_____
PRICE RANGE_____
GENERAL APPEARANCE OF PROPERTIES IN THE VICINITY _____
_____

Contractor Information Form

Company Name:_____   Phone: (   ) _____
Contact Name: _____   Phone: (   ) _____
Address: _____   Fax: (   ) _____

Number of years in business? _____

Number of FULL-TIME employees? _____   PART-TIME? _____

The majority of your business is conducted in what county?_____

The majority of your business is conducted in what town? _____

How much advance notice is generally required before starting a job? _____

Are you a General Contractor?   Yes [ ]   No [   ]
Are you a member of your state Builder's Association?   Yes [ ]   No [   ]
Does your company offer liability insurance?   Yes [ ]   No [   ]
      Carrier Name:_____   Policy no._____

Does your company offer workman's compensation?   Yes [ ]   No [   ]
      Carrier Name:_____   Policy no._____

Are you State Licensed in any of the following areas: Electrical   Yes [ ]   No [   ]
Plumbing   Yes [ ]   No [   ]   Heating & A/C   Yes [ ]   No [   ]

Are any of the following areas specialties or areas of interest:

Paving	Yes [ ]	No [ ]	Siding	Yes [ ]	No [ ]	
Masonry	Yes [ ]	No [ ]	Trim work	Yes [ ]	No [ ]	
Decks/Porches	Yes [ ]	No [ ]	Taping & Spackling	Yes [ ]	No [ ]	
Foundation	Yes [ ]	No [ ]	Painting	Yes [ ]	No [ ]	
Framing	Yes [ ]	No [ ]	Paper Hanging	Yes [ ]	No [ ]	
Insulation	Yes [ ]	No [ ]	Kitchen Remodeling	Yes [ ]	No [ ]	
Roofing	Yes [ ]	No [ ]	Bathroom Remodeling	Yes [ ]	No [ ]	
Drywall	Yes [ ]	No [ ]	Total Rehabilitation	Yes [ ]	No [ ]	

Would you be interested in purchasing Invtmt property requiring renovation?
                                                          Yes [ ]   No [   ]
Please list 3 business references:
1- _____
2- _____
3- _____

Please provide any additional information that will assist us in making a decision:
_____
_____
_____

Signed by: _____   Date:_____

Purchase Offer Form

DATE:_____

BUYER and/or ASSIGNEES:_____

ADDRESS:_____

HEREBY AGREES TO PURCHASE FROM

SELLER:_____

ADDRESS:_____

THROUGH_____

(listing/selling broker)

AT PRICE AND TERMS STATED BELOW, THE PREMISES LOCATED AT:

ADDRESS:_____

ALSO KNOWN AS LOT(S):_____ BLOCK:_____ AS SHOWN ON

THE TAX MAP OF _____, COUNTY OF _____

PAYMENT OF THE PURCHASE PRICE IS AS FOLLOWS:

PURCHASE PRICE	$_____
DEPOSIT HEREWITH, FOR WHICH THIS IS A RECEIPT	$_____
ADDITIONAL DEPOSIT UPON COMPLETION OF ATTORNEY REVIEW	$_____
MORTGAGE AMOUNT	$_____
ASSUME EXISTING MORTGAGE	$_____
SELLER TO TAKE BACK A NOTE AND MORTGAGE	$_____
BALANCE PAID AT CLOSING WITH CERTIFIED FUNDS	$_____

CLOSING DATE: **30 Days After Completion of Attorney Review**

OFFER IS SUBJECT TO THE FOLLOWING CONTINGENCIES:

Inspection of the Property. The Seller agrees to permit the Buyer to perform inspections, including, but not limited to: engineering inspection, wood-destroying insect inspection, radon inspection, well and septic inspections. The buyer will pay for these inspection. In the event that the results of such inspections do not meet with the Buyer's approval, for any reason, the buyer may cancel this Offer To Purchase with the return of all deposit monies. Said inspections are to be performed within ten (10) business days from the written approval of this Offer To Purchase. Seller agrees to permit access for all inspections provided for in this Offer To Purchase.

BROKERS COMMISSSION: <u>N/A</u>   As Per Listing Agreement

This offer to purchase is subject to the approval and acceptance of _____
Within 72 hours of receipt.

BUYER AGREES TO PURCHASE SUBJECT PROPERTY AT THE ABOVE SAID PRICE & TERMS

_____	_____	_____	_____
SELLER	DATE	BUYER	DATE

_____	_____	_____	_____
SELLER	DATE	BUYER	DATE

THE BUYER AND SELLER ACKNOWLEDGE THAT THIS IS AN OFFER TO PURCHASE AND IS SUBJECT TO THE EXECUTION OF CONTRACT TO PURCHASE.

BWIC Property Management, Inc.'s
DOUBLE YOUR INCOME THRU Real Estate Investment:
MENTOR COMMITMENT CONTRACT

I _____, understand and abide to the following criteria and stipulation in joining the DOUBLE YOUR INCOME.

I will be available, at the same telephone number, for all scheduled DOUBLE YOUR INCOME calls.

I will participate and complete my program for all 12 ½ hour scheduled calls.

I will be open to coaching and will apply the teachings of my DOUBLE YOUR INCOME Coach.

I will be available and participate in all accountability calls with my accountability partner.

I understand that if I choose to cancel my program for any reason I will still be held accountable to and responsible for paying for the balance of the program in full.

If I choose to put my program on hold for any reason, I will continue to make payments to BWIC Property Management, Inc. and will complete the program within 15 months of the first call.

_____   _____

Client Signature   Date_

The authors, its agents and assigns, specifically disclaim any liability, loss or risk, personal or otherwise, incurred as a consequence directly or indirectly of the use and/or application of the techniques and/or materials provided in this program. These materials are published for educational purposes only. This information is provided to program participants as additional personal financial strategies. These materials are intended to enable participants to engage in commercial activities or to start or augment a business.

The content in this program are provided for educational purposes. The information may not be appropriate for use in all states. Therefore, you should request that your professional adviser review these, or any other forms you plan to use for any purpose.

BWIC Property Management, Inc.
P.O. Box 304907
St. Thomas, V.I. 00803

Email: bwic777@yahoo.com
www.busyrealestateinvestor.com
Phone: 340-227-9637
E-fax: 305-397-2516

If you received this document from anyone else other than www.busyrealestateinvestor.com it is stolen. We offer a cash reward to anyone who reports such theft. Please report all theft to: bwic777@ yahoo.com

Printed in the United States
by Baker & Taylor Publisher Services